Welcome to the World!

Carson-Dellosa's *A Trip Around the World* gives you and your students the opportunity to explore life in Mexico, Brazil, Egypt, Kenya, Germany, The Netherlands, Saudi Arabia, China, Japan, Australia, Canada, and The United States. The section for each country contains basic information (area, population, flag descriptions, etc.), fascinating facts (sports, education, wildlife, etc.), language activities, recipes, classroom activities, flags, maps, a worksheet, and a resource list. Below are lists of expansion ideas for each type of activity provided in each country:

Basic Information
- Use the Almanac information to make comparisons. For example, how many Mexican pesos will equal an American dollar?
- Discuss the countries' histories. Have the native cultures had similar experiences?
- Use the cover and flag descriptions to compare similarities in the countries' flags. How many have religious or mythical elements, how many have undergone changes through the years, etc.?
- After studying the flags of each country, have your students pretend they are forming a new country. Have cooperative groups come up with samples for a flag and have them explain the reasoning behind their design. Have the class vote on the design they want to represent their new country.
- Have the children invite their grandparents to tell stories about the history of their family's original homeland. Have them share their experiences.
- Graph the types of land formations found in each country. How many countries have deserts, tropical zones, etc.?
- Make a list of all the natural resources that are cultivated in each country. Have your students discuss the resources in those countries that are imported by the United States. Can they name one from each country? The students could also discuss what life would be like for our country and other countries if we didn't have certain resources.

Fascinating Facts
- Write the fascinating facts of each country on 3" x 5" index cards. Laminate them. Use the cards to play a trivia game.
- Create customary art from each country described in this section. Have your students make a piñata, origami, Chinese lanterns, etc.
- Use the information as topics for oral or written reports. The students could even do a comparison study (sports from two countries, etc.).
- Find pictures of houses or buildings mentioned in this section or the basic information section. Assign a group of students to each country. Have them build replicas with ice cream sticks, papier-mâché, grass, straw, clay, etc. Use the buildings to make a global neighborhood.

Language Activities
- Have your students create coded messages using some of each country's language. Have them pick partners and trade messages.
- Practice using the languages each day. Can the students use the words in conversation?
- Create file folder games with the different categories of words. Have the students match up all the color words, ways to say hello, etc. File folders can be used to match flags, maps of countries, types of money, etc., as well.

Recipes
- Copy the recipes in each section and send one home with each child. Have them make the recipe with their parents and bring it to school the next day for a multicultural snack time. Host an international-snack party for another class.

- Have a multicultural bake sale. Have students and their families bake their favorite international dish. Sell the goods and donate the money raised to an international charity organization.

Classroom Activities
- Have each student make a family tree as far back as possible. Post the trees around the room. Do any of the students have ancestors from any of the countries studied in this book?
- Locate schools in the countries you're studying. Contact one of the schools and see if it is willing to start a pen-pal program with your class. Contact the country's embassy for more information.
- Make-up story starters for your class. For example, "My favorite country is _____, because _____," or "I visited _____ and I saw_____."
- Host a multicultural festival with food, music, dancing, and celebrations from all the countries. Invite the whole school. Make it a yearly event.
- Research one of the countries in depth as a class. When you have gathered all the research, have your students help you put all the information into a book. Donate the book to your school library. Encourage other classrooms to do the same with other countries. Give your students assignments that will encourage them to use the books they helped make.

Flags
- Have a parade of nations. Have the class dress in native costumes made from fabric scraps, beads, etc. Have each child make a flag for the country he is dressed to represent.
- Have each student design a flag to represent himself.
- Enlarge, reproduce, color, and mount the flags on tagboard. Post flags around the room. Borrow a copy of a national athems record from your local library. Have the students pick a flag to salute each morning and play that country's anthem. You can even learn the words and sing along.
- Have a mock-United Nations meeting with all the flags and countries present. Try solving global problems that are currently in the news.
- Make floor puzzles from the flags. Enlarge, color, cut out, and mount on tagboard. Cut the flag into puzzle pieces.

Maps
- Enlarge the maps to use as pages for a shape book. Use the pages to list cities, resources, topographical regions, ethnic backgrounds, etc.
- Enlarge and trace onto cardboard. Use plaster of Paris, clay, or papier-mâché to create a topographical map of the country. You can add animals in appropriate places as well as natural resources and industries.

Worksheets
- Use the sheets to make file folder games.
- Use the reproducibles to make finger puppets, necklaces, shape books, etc.

Resource List
- While studying a certain country, have a student help you read one of the books each day to the class.
- Have the students pretend they are the main characters in the books. How would they react to American customs? How do they like being in the characters' shoes?
- Use the books to compare national holidays. Compare the ways other countries celebrate Christmas, Easter, Ramadan, Carnival, Chinese New Year, etc., to how Americans celebrate these holidays.
- Read folktales from all the countries. Discuss their similarities and differences. Have the students make up their own folktales.

First Stop...Mexico

Area: 761,604 sq. miles
Capital City: Mexico City
Population: 113,724,226
Main Language: Spanish
Main Religion: Roman Catholicism
Currency: Mexican Peso
Government: Federal Republic
Flag:

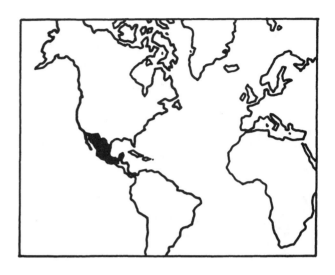

The national flag has three vertical bands. From left to right they are green, white, and red. Green stands for independence, white stands for religion, and red stands for union. The coat of arms in the center illustrates an Aztec legend that explains the founding of Mexico City.

For Your Information

Mexico is located on the continent of North America. Its neighbor to the north is the United States. Guatemala and Belize border Mexico to the south. The Pacific Ocean is west of Mexico, and he Gulf of Mexico is to the east. Mexico has two large peninsulas. The Yucatan Peninsula forms the eastern end of Mexico. The Baja California Peninsula is on Mexico's western coast. "The Baja" has dry desert areas and high mountains. It is almost 800 miles long and is one of the longest peninsulas in the world.

Most people living in Mexico are part Spanish and part Native Mexican. For thousands of years, the Native Mexicans were the only people in Mexico. In 1519, Spain began to conquer Mexico. Over many years, the Spanish and Native Mexican cultures have blended to form the rich culture of Mexico.

For thousands of years, corn has been the most important crop in Mexico. Farmers make up approximately one-fifth of the Mexican population. Today, many farmers are trying to immigrate to the United States in search of work, because they can't find work in the overcrowded cities of Mexico.

Fascinating Facts

In Mexico, children are given both their father's last name and the mother's maiden name. For example, if a child whose first name is Carlos, has a father named Juan Gonzáles and a mother named Luisa Garcia, the child is then called Carlos Gonzáles Garcia. This Mexican custom of naming children helps preserve the heritage of both parents.

Some Mexicans use **adobe**, a mixture of wet clay and straw, to build houses. On hot days, adobe walls keep cooler temperatures inside the house.

Mexico's land is composed of mountains, deserts, and tropical zones. There are three mountain ranges; all of them are named Sierra Madre. Two of the ranges run down each side of Mexico's coastlines and the third runs between the coasts on the southern end of Mexico just below Mexico City.

The ancient Aztec city of Tenochtitlán was built in 1325, and was destroyed by the Spanish when they conquered Mexico. It is now the site of Mexico City, the capital of Mexico.

When the Spanish army arrived in Mexico in 1519, Mexico was inhabited by over 700 Indian tribes.

Before the war between Mexico and the United States (1846), Mexico's territory included all of Texas, California, Nevada, and Utah; and parts of Colorado, New Mexico, and Wyoming.

In 1862, Napoleon III attempted to invade Mexico. His army was defeated by the Mexican forces on May 5, 1867, at the Battle of Puebla. Mexicans still celebrate the victory, or Cinco de Mayo, every fifth of May with parades, piñatas, and dances.

The tortilla, Mexico's most famous bread, is an unleavened corn or flour cake. Preparation includes soaking the corn kernels in limewater until they are soft enough to grind, and then adding water, a little at a time, to make the dough. The dough is rolled until it is very thin and then it is baked.

Language Activities

Colors

rojo (row-ho)	red
azul (as-ool)	blue
amarillo (ah-ma-ree-yo)	yellow
verde (vehr-day)	green
anaranjado	orange
(a-nar-an-ha-dough)	
rosado (row-sa-dough)	pink
marrón (ma-rone)	brown
blanco (blan-co)	white
negro (nay-grow)	black

Spanish Numbers

uno (oon-o) --one
dos (doss)--two
tres (tress)--three
cuatro (kwa-tro)--four
cinco (seen-ko)--five
seis (sseyss)--six
siete (ssyete)--seven
ocho (o-cho)--eight
nueve (nwe-be)--nine
dies (deeyes)--ten

Days of the Week

lunes (loon-ez)
martes (mar-tez)
miércoles (me-air-ko-lez)
jueves (whe-vez)
viernes (vi-air-nez)
sábado (sa-ba-dó)
domingo (doh-min-go)

*Days are listed Monday-Sunday

Everyday Spanish Expressions

hola (o-la)	hello
buenos días (bwe-noos de-yass)	good day
por favor (poor fah-vohr)	please
adiós (a-dee-oss)	good-bye
¿Cómo te llamas? (coh-mow tay yah-mahs)	What is your name?
¿Cuántos años tienes? (kwan-tows anyos tee-yn-ays)	How old are you?
¿Cómo estas? (coh-mow ay-stahs)	How are you?
Muy bien, gracias. (mooee bee-ain grah-see-ahs)	I am fine, thank you.
¿Habla ingles? (ah-blah eeng-lace)	Do you speak English?

Music

Mexican children sing the following song, "Buenos Días," to the tune of "Happy Birthday."

Buenos días a ustedes,	Good morning to you,
Buenos días a ustedes,	Good morning to you,
Buenos días, buenos días,	Good morning, good morning,
Buenos días a ustedes.	Good morning to you.

Mexican Recipe

Tortillas

Ingredients:
4 cups of corn, wheat or white flour
¾ cup hot water
1 tsp. salt
1 cup shortening

Directions:
Mix flour, salt and shortening. Add hot water a little at a time (more than ¾ cup may be needed). Mix until firm and let stand. Roll a heaping tablespoon of the dough with a rolling pin until it is smooth and thin. Cook on a hot griddle over a low flame until moderately brown. Butter and serve as bread with a meal or as a snack.

Classroom Activities

- Have the children assume Mexican names for a day, or have the children find out what their name would be in the Mexican custom of preserving the heritage of both parents.

- Have a Mexican feast! Make the flour tortillas on page 6, and enjoy them with other Mexican foods including tacos, fajitas, and burritos.

- Celebrate Cinco de Mayo (any time of year will do, but May 5th is best) with colorful costumes, piñatas, and tissue paper flowers (see directions on page 8) as decorations. Provide the children with a sombrero and let them make up a version of the Mexican hat dance.

- Explore Mexico's diverse land by making a topographical map out of cardboard, clay, and any other creative materials to show the water masses, the peninsulas, the dry deserts, and the high mountains.

- In cooperative groups, have the children make adobe houses using clay shaped into small cubes as building blocks. Let the houses dry in the sun.

- Decorate the classroom with Mexican art. Use the tissue-paper flower directions on page 8.

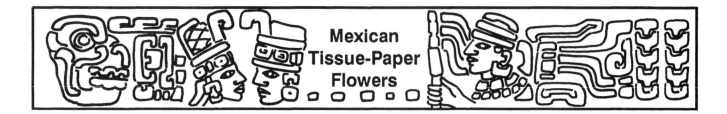

1. Take six sheets of tissue paper and fold them like a fan. You can use several different colors for each flower, or you can make a solidly-colored flower.

2. Cut the folded paper in half. Each half will make one flower.

3. Take one half at a time, still folded, and trim both ends into a broad point.

4. Bend a twist tie around the center of each folded strip of paper.

5. Gently separate each layer of the folded paper by pulling upwards and downwards until you have formed a circular shape.

6. Tape the ends together at the top and bottom so the flower will stay open.

7. Decorate your classroom with lots of these flowers. Have your students make collages, pictures, paintings, diaramas, etc., showing what they have learned about Mexico. Invite another class, the principal, and parents to view your Mexican Art Gallery.

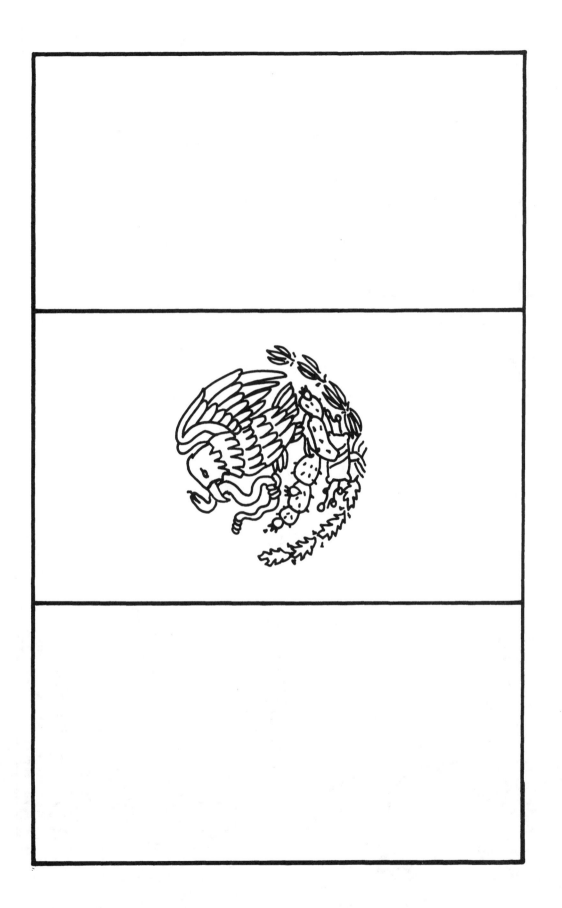

THE FLAG OF MEXICO

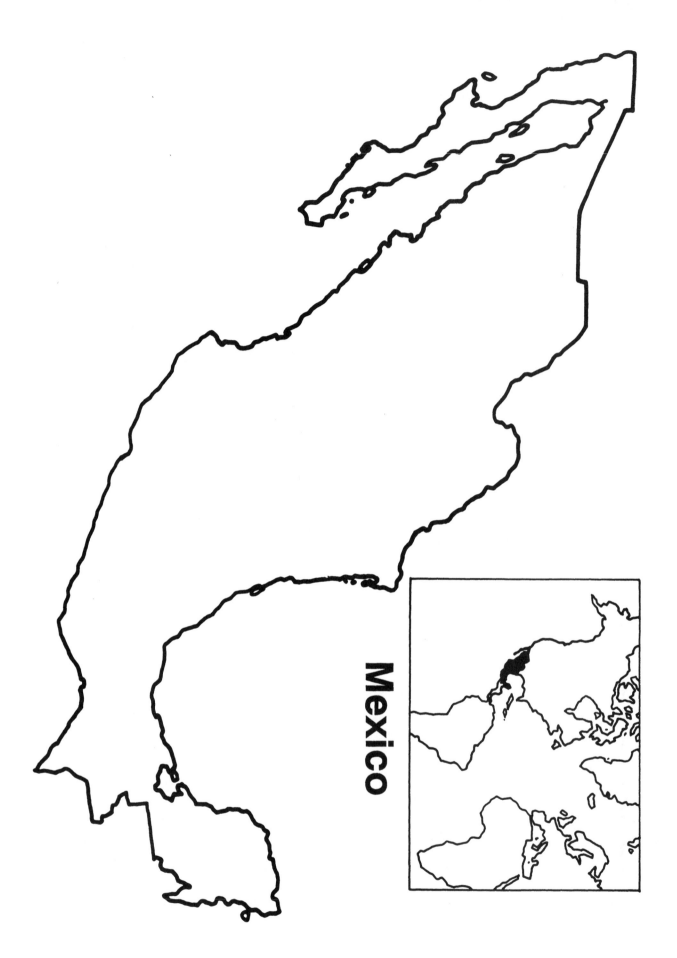

Mexico

10

Name _____

Los Colores
Colors

Directions: Have your students color the sombreros correctly after you've discussed the color words in class. Enlarge them and use for pages of a Mexican book of colors. Cut out and attach the hats to stick puppets. Have the puppets dance around a paper hat for a Mexican hat dance.

rojo (red)   azul (blue)   amarillo (yellow)

verde (green)   anaranjado (orange) rosado (pink)

marrón (brown)   blanco (white)   negro (black)

11

Teacher Resources

Ancona, George. *El piñatero/ The Piñata Maker.* Harcourt Paperbacks, 1994.

Brown, Tricia. *Hello Amigos!* Henry Holt & Co., 1992.

Casagrande, L. and Johnson, Sylvia A. *Focus on Mexico: Modern Life in an Ancient Land.* Lerner Publ. Co., 1986.

Coronado, Rosa. *Cooking the Mexican Way.* Lerner Publ. Co., 2001.

Fisher, Angela. *Pyramids of the Sun, Pyramid of the Moon.* Atheneum, 1988.

Garza, Carmen Lomas. *In My Family/En mi familia.* Children's Book Press, 2000.

Haskins, J. *Count Your Way Through Mexico.* Carolrhoda Books, 1989.

Harvey, Miles. *Look What Came from Mexico!* Franklin Watts, 1999.

Heiman, Sarah. *Mexico ABCs: A Book About the People and Places of Mexico.* Picture Window Books, 2002.

Heinrichs, Ann. *Mexico* (*True Books*). Children's Press, 1997.

Irizarry, C. *Passport to Mexico.* Franklin Watts, 1994.

Johnston, Tony. *My Mexico/México mío.* Putnam Juvenile, 1999.

Kalman, Bobbie and Lewis, Jane. *Mexico from A to Z.* Crabtree Publishing Co., 1999.

Milford, Susan. *Mexico: 40 Activities to Experience Mexico Past and Present.* Williamson Publishing Co., 1999.

Olawsky, Lynn Ainsworth. *Colors of Mexico.* Carolrhoda Books, 1997.

Rohmer, Harriet. *The Legend of Food Mountain.* Children's Press, 1982.

Turck, Mary C. *Mexico and Central America: A Fiesta of Cultures, Crafts, and Activities for Ages 8–12.* Chicago Review Press, 2004.

Wade, Mary Dodson. *Cinco de Mayo.* Children's Press, 2003.

Winter, Jeanette. *Diego.* Sagebrush, 1999.

Landing in Brazil

Area: 3,286,470 sq. miles
Capital City: Brasilia
Population: 186,112,794
Main Language: Portuguese
Main Religion: Roman Catholicism
Currency: Real
Government: Federal Republic
Flag:

Brazil's national flag displays its motto, "Order and Progress." The background is green and the diamond is yellow. Green and yellow represent agricultural and mineral resources. The blue of the globe and the white of the stars represent Brazil's ties to Portugal. The stars represent the states.

For Your Information

Brazil is located on the continent of South America. It is the fifth largest country in the world and makes up nearly half of the total area of South America. Brazil borders every country in South America except Chile and Ecuador. The climate is temperate in the southern region, and most of the major cities are located there. The northern region of Brazil has a tropical climate and is almost entirely covered by the world's largest rain forest, the Amazon. The destruction of Brazil's rain forests has become a major environmental issue. This destruction threatens many plant and animal species with extinction. Environmentalists are working hard to protect Brazil's endangered rain forests.

Portugal claimed Brazil in 1500 even though Brazil was already inhabited by Native South Americans. Colonists from Portugal built large sugar plantations and brought many African slaves with them to work the plantations. In 1888, slavery was abolished in Brazil. Many of the remaining Native South Americans today live in the forests along the banks of the Amazon River. The Portuguese spoken in Brazil has been greatly influenced by the African and Native South American dialects present during the colonization of Brazil.

Fascinating Facts

 The rain forest of Brazil has five layers: **forest floor, shrub, understory, canopy, and emergent**. Each layer is important to the growth of the entire rain forest.

Some of the rain forest's rare and wonderful creatures include the following: the caiman crocodile, the morpho butterfly, the spotted ocelot, seven-foot river otter, the emerald boa, and many colorful flowers.

 It rains about seven feet a year in the Amazon basin of Brazil.

The Amazon River is the second longest river in the world. It is 4,000 miles long and its basin covers 2,700,000 square miles.

Tropical fruit, like bananas, melons, pineapples, mangoes, and oranges, are grown throughout Brazil. Almost every Brazilian meal includes some fruit.

 Cocoa has been a favorite drink of Brazilians for hundreds of years. Cocoa and chocolate come from the beans of the cacao tree.

 Carnival is one of the most exciting festivals in Brazil. Carnival begins the Saturday before Lent and lasts until the following Tuesday. During the festival, Brazilians express their national pride and identity through masquerades, parades, dancing, and theme parties.

 Futebol (soccer) is the national sport of Brazil. One of the best known soccer players in the world, Pelé, is from Brazil.

The seasons in Brazil are opposite from those in North America because South America is in the Southern Hemisphere. For example, when the Brazilians celebrate Christmas, it is warm instead of cold.

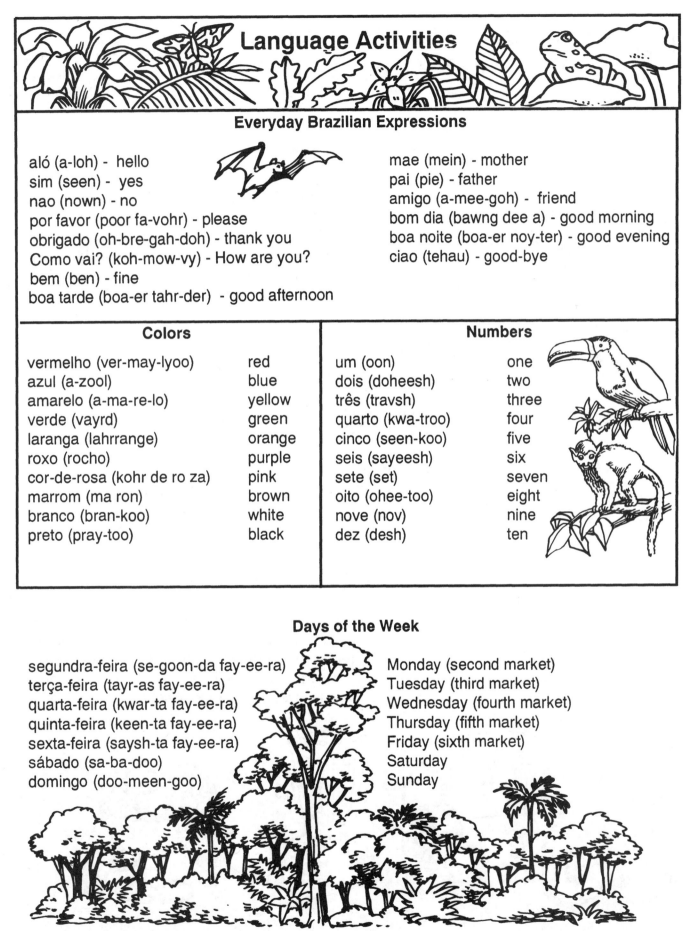

Language Activities

Everyday Brazilian Expressions

aló (a-loh) - hello
sim (seen) - yes
nao (nown) - no
por favor (poor fa-vohr) - please
obrigado (oh-bre-gah-doh) - thank you
Como vai? (koh-mow-vy) - How are you?
bem (ben) - fine
boa tarde (boa-er tahr-der) - good afternoon

mae (mein) - mother
pai (pie) - father
amigo (a-mee-goh) - friend
bom dia (bawng dee a) - good morning
boa noite (boa-er noy-ter) - good evening
ciao (tehau) - good-bye

Colors

vermelho (ver-may-lyoo)	red
azul (a-zool)	blue
amarelo (a-ma-re-lo)	yellow
verde (vayrd)	green
laranga (lahrrange)	orange
roxo (rocho)	purple
cor-de-rosa (kohr de ro za)	pink
marrom (ma ron)	brown
branco (bran-koo)	white
preto (pray-too)	black

Numbers

um (oon)	one
dois (doheesh)	two
três (travsh)	three
quarto (kwa-troo)	four
cinco (seen-koo)	five
seis (sayeesh)	six
sete (set)	seven
oito (ohee-too)	eight
nove (nov)	nine
dez (desh)	ten

Days of the Week

segundra-feira (se-goon-da fay-ee-ra)	Monday (second market)
terça-feira (tayr-as fay-ee-ra)	Tuesday (third market)
quarta-feira (kwar-ta fay-ee-ra)	Wednesday (fourth market)
quinta-feira (keen-ta fay-ee-ra)	Thursday (fifth market)
sexta-feira (saysh-ta fay-ee-ra)	Friday (sixth market)
sábado (sa-ba-doo)	Saturday
domingo (doo-meen-goo)	Sunday

Brazilian Recipes

Brigaderiros (A Chocolate Treat)

Ingredients:
2 tablespoons margarine
1 can (14 oz.) sweetened, condensed milk
2 tablespoons baking cocoa
chocolate sprinkles

Directions:
Mix the margarine, condensed milk, and the cocoa together. Cook over low heat, stirring continuously until thick. Remove from heat and cool completely. Grease your hands with margarine and roll the chocolate into small balls. Roll the ball in the chocolate sprinkles.

Abacate Batido (Whipped Avocado Dessert)

Ingredients:
4 ripe avocados
½ cup whipping cream
⅔ cup powdered sugar
6 tablespoons lime juice

Directions:
Cut avocados into pieces. Put the avocados and remaining ingredients into a blender and blend until smooth. Serve in dessert cups and garnish with lime wedges. Serves eight.

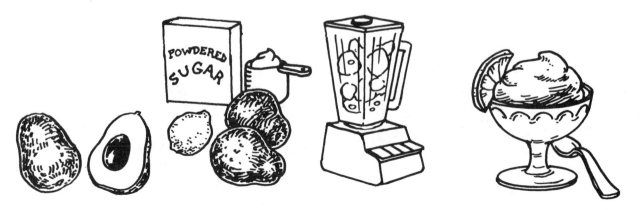

Classroom Activities

Have the class research information about the different layers of the rain forest. In cooperative groups, each student can illustrate a layer. Then, they can explain to the class how each layer is important to the entire rain forest. The students can also study the rare animals in the Brazilian rain forests.

Integrate the study of Brazil with other disciplines by having the students raise funds to save the Amazon Rain Forest. Your class can sell bags of popcorn before school, have a bake sale, create and sell "Save the Rain Forest" buttons, or simply collect donations. All funds collected can be sent to an environmental group involved with saving the rain forests.

Have a Brazilian Carnival in your classroom complete with colorful costumes, decorations, music, and dancing. The children can make decorations to hang from the ceiling. You may want to hold a contest to judge the best decorations and the best costumes. Teach your students the Brazilian Carnival Dance. You can find this song (directions for the dance are the lyrics to the song) on *Children of the World* by Georgiana Stewart. (published by Kimbo Educational Records, Long Branch, NJ, 1991).

Soccer is the national sport of Brazil. Play soccer with your class during recess or P. E. (don't forget to call it futebol).

Introduce time-telling skills while studying Brazil. Use the song "Tico Tico Counting Song" from *Multicultural Rhythm Sticks* by Georgiana Stewart (published by Kimbo Educational Records, Long Branch, NJ, 1992). Your students can practice their rhythm, motor, and time-telling skills to a Brazilian samba beat.

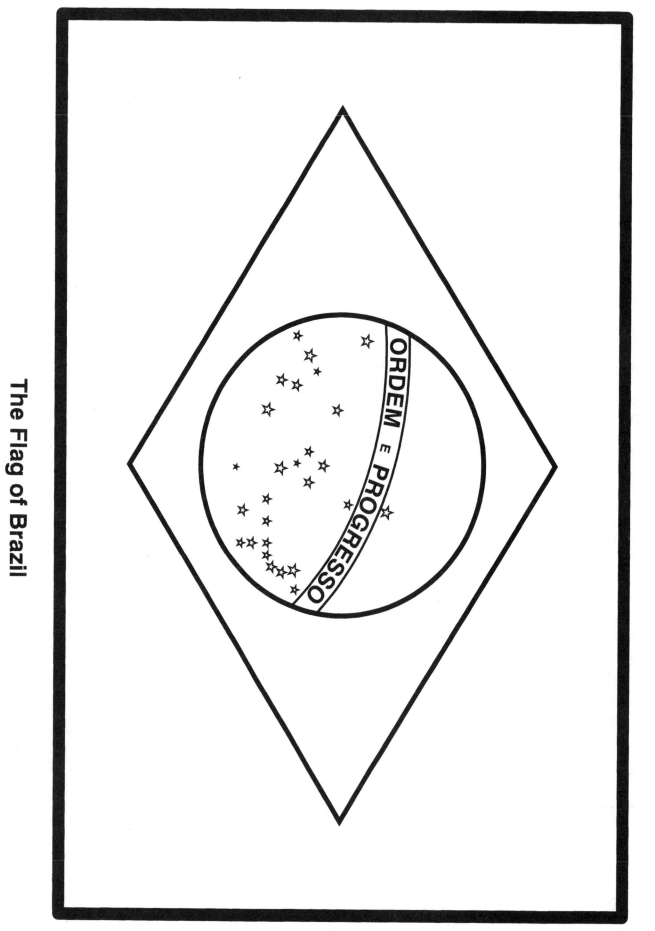

The Flag of Brazil

18

Brazil

19

Name _____

Brazilian Crossword

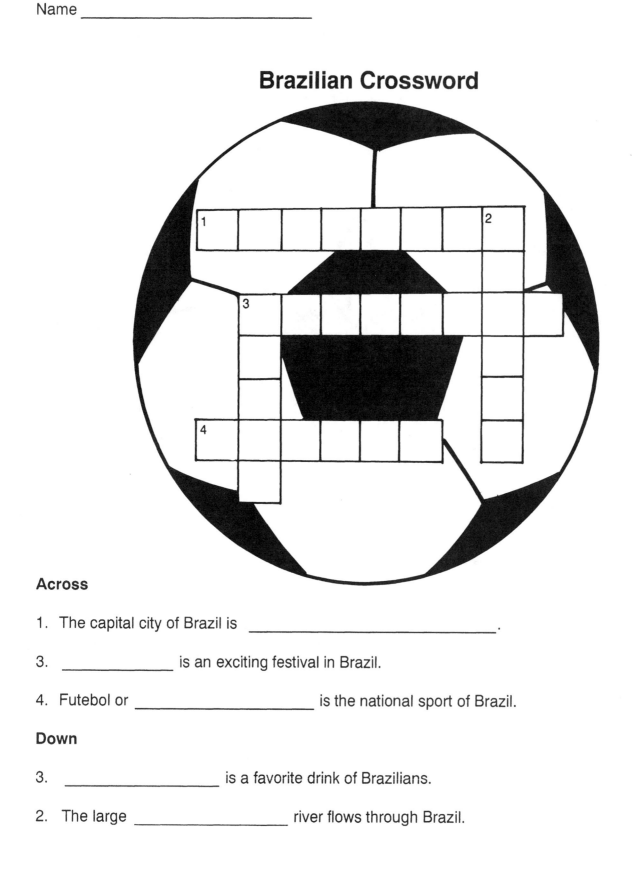

Across

1. The capital city of Brazil is _____.

3. _____ is an exciting festival in Brazil.

4. Futebol or _____ is the national sport of Brazil.

Down

3. _____ is a favorite drink of Brazilians.

2. The large _____ river flows through Brazil.

Teacher Resources

Baker, Lucy. *Life in the Rain Forests*. Sagebrush, 2002.

Black, Carolyn and Hollander, Malika. *Brazil: The Culture*. Crabtree Publishing Co., 2003.

Brown, Rose. *The Land and People of Brazil*. HarperCollins, 1979.

Canizares, Susan and Chessen, Betsey. *Rainforest Colors*. Scholastic, 1998.

Cherry, Lynne. *The Great Kapok Tree*. Voyager Books, 2000.

Delacre, Lulu. *Golden Tales: Myths, Legends and Folktales From Latin America*. Scholastic, 2001.

DeSpain, Pleasant. *Dancing Turtle: Folktale from Brazil*. August House Publishers, 1998.

Fontes, Justine and Fontes, Ron. *Brazil*. Scholastic, 2004.

Gerson, Mary-Joan. *How Night Came From the Sea: A Story From Brazil*. Little, Brown & Co., 1994.

Gibbons, Gail. *Nature's Green Umbrella*. HarperTrophy, 1997.

Goalec, Francois. *Frederico: A Child of Brazil*. Blackbirch Press, 2005.

Haskins, James and Benson, Kathleen. *Count Your Way Through Brazil*. Lerner Publ. Co., 1996.

Hays, Peter and Rozen, Beti. *Stolen Spirit*. Sem Fronteiras Press, 2000.

Heinrichs, Ann. *Brazil*. Scholastic, 1997.

Machado, Ana Maria. *From Another World*. Groundwood Books, 2006.

Silver, Donald M. *Tropical Rain Forest*. McGraw-Hill, 1998.

Arriving in Egypt

Area: 386,650 sq. miles
Capital City: Cairo
Population: 82,079,636
Main Language: Arabic
Main Religion: Islam
Currency: Egyptian Pound
Government: Republic
Flag:

The Egyptian flag has three horizontal bands with the colors red, white, and black. The eagle in the middle is a symbol of Saladin, a Muslim warrior who lived during the 1100's. The panel below the eagle bears the country's name.

For Your Information

Egypt is located in the northeastern corner of Africa. It is considered a middle easter country because of its religious, cultural, and commercial ties to the Mediterranean. The majority of Egyptians are Muslim like their Middle Eastern neighbors. Little rain falls in Egypt and most of the country is covered by the Sahara Desert. About 99 percent of all Egyptians live along the Nile River Valley and the Suez Canal. Cairo, Egypt's capital, is the largest city in both Africa and the Arab world.

The Egyptians who live in cities reside in private homes, apartment houses, and crowded tenement districts. They work in occupations that are similar to those found in most cities. Half of the people in Egypt are peasants, called **fellahin** (fellah is the singular form), who live in rural areas. Most of the fellahin work much like their ancestors did by farming cotton or growing rice, oranges, and sugar cane. However, many of the people have moved from rural villages to the cities in search of work. As a result, the cities of Egypt have become overcrowded.

Egypt has a history dating back over 51,000 years. The ancient Egyptians developed the world's first government and early forms of writing and mathematics. Ancient Egypt is best known for the great pyramids built as tombs for its rulers. The most famous pyramids stand at Giza and so does the Great Sphinx, the most popular statue of its kind.

Fascinating Facts

To irrigate their farms, the Egyptians use an ancient tool called a **shadoof**. It is a type of lever that dips the water out of the Nile River and into the irrigation troughs.

The Nile River is very important to Egypt for irrigation, transportation, and food. In ancient Egypt, life revolved around the river's annual rise and fall. After flooding, rich silt remained and left fertile ground for growing grapes, wheat, and other crops.

Our modern calendar has been somewhat influenced by the Egyptian Calendar. The Egyptians created a twelve month, 365-day calendar. Unlike our calendar, each month had thirty days and every week had ten days. The gods were honored with sacrifices and celebrations on the remaining five days.

Papyrus was the earliest form of paper. The Egyptians made the paper by using the papyrus reed that grew along the banks of the Nile.

Hieroglyphics (Greek for "sacred carvings") was an ancient form of writing. There were more than 700 symbols (called hieroglyphs) which appear on tombs, temples, and other monuments. In the early 1800's, Jean Francois Champollion, a Frenchman, deciphered the Hieroglyphic code from the Rosetta Stone.

Pharaohs, or rulers, had a profound effect on ancient Egypt. A pharaoh's most important duty was to establish truth, order, and justice throughout the land. The pharaoh's word was law.

The pyramids of Egypt were built over a span of one thousand years and were made of limestone and granite. The Great Pyramid of Khufu is one of the seven wonders of the ancient world.

The early Egyptians had a strong belief in immortality. The huge pyramids were built as tombs for the pharaohs. The Egyptians used mummification to preserve the bodies and to ensure the eternal life of the soul. Personal belongings were placed in the tombs for use in the afterlife. Unfortunately, grave-robbers often vandalized the tombs in search of treasures.

One of the most famous tombs is that of King Tutankhamen (commonly known as King Tut). He became a ruler at age nine and it is believed he died at age 18. The treasures of King Tut were found in 1922 by British archeologist Howard Carter.

The Great Sphinx of Giza is the largest statue to survive from ancient times. It has the head of a man and the body of a lion. Historians believed that the head was built to look like King Khafre, and that the lion's body stood for the king's strength. Unlike the pyramids, the Great Sphnix was not built for burial.

Language Activities

Directions: Below are some examples of hieroglyphs. Have your students make up their own symbols. Have them make up symbols for friendship, health, family, nature, etc. Have them make up symbols to represent themselves. Have your students share their "hieroglyphics" with each other. Have them write stories using symbols. Can their friends and parents read it?

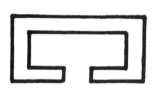

woman   a reed leaf   a foot   an owl   a sedgelike plant

a house   a hoe   a basket   liquids

a field shelter   a lion   a plow   a kid

Egyptian Recipes

Honeyed Carrots

Ingredients:
24 carrots, sliced
⅔ cup honey
4 tablespoons vegetable oil
2 teaspoons lemon juice
1 teaspoon salt

Directions:
Boil 4 inches of salted water in a large saucepan. Add sliced carrots to the boiling water. Cover and cook for about 20 minutes or until tender. Drain. In a skillet, cook the remaining ingredients until bubbly. Add carrots. Cook uncovered over low heat for about three minutes or until carrots are covered evenly with the glaze.

Palace Bread (*Aish al-seraya*)

Ingredients:
2 sticks butter
2 cups honey
1 cup bread crumbs
whipped cream or ice cream

Directions:
Heat butter and honey until mixture thickens. Add bread crumbs and cook for about 20 minutes, stirring frequently. Put mixture on a plate and let it cool. Cut into triangles and top with whipped cream or ice cream.

Have your students make a model pyramid:

Directions:
1. Using construction paper or cardboard, cut an 8 ½" square (see fig. a).
2. Make a mark at the midpoint of each side (4 ¼"). Connect the opposite points by drawing a large cross (see fig. b).
3. From the center of the square, measure 3 ¼" out along each cross line and place a mark at each of the four locations. Draw lines to connect each corner of the paper to the new 3 ¼" marks.
4. Cut along the new lines (see fig. c).
5. Fold along the lines that form a square shown in figure d. Tape or glue the edges together (see fig. d).
6. You now have a pyramid! You may want to decorate your pyramid by drawing stones or hieroglyphs.

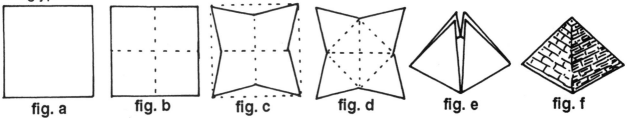

| fig. a | fig. b | fig. c | fig. d | fig. e | fig. f |

In cooperative groups, make the Pyramids of Giza out of sugar cubes. You will need a few boxes of cubes and heavy pieces of cardboard (for the base). This activity will help demonstrate the unique shape of pyramids, square on the bottom and triangular on the sides. It is also an excellent preparation for basic geometry.

Have the children make their own Rosetta Stone. Pour plaster of Paris (follow mixing directions on the box) into individual foam meat trays. When the mixture dries, the students can use large nails to carve hieroglyphics (or their own patterns) into the stone. This activity should be done with close adult supervision. If you prefer, you can roll out soft clay into the meat trays. Students can carve their hieroglyphs with ice cream sticks or the ends of paint brushes.

Learn more about the ancient dress and appearances of the Egyptians. Have the children help each other trace the outlines of their bodies onto large pieces of butcher paper. Let the children draw Egyptian costumes for themselves.

Pick different children to be pharaohs for the day or hour. Have the student establish truth, order, and justice in his or her own way. Afterwards, have a classroom discussion. Did the class like having a pharaoh? What were some of the problems, if any? What were the best and worst things about being pharaoh? Do you think pharaohs would be good rulers today?

As a class group, have a discussion about Egyptian tombs. Bring in a big box and let the students decorate it with hieroglyphs. Then pick a famous ancient Egyptian and have the students decide what he or she would need on the journey to the afterlife. Discuss archaeology and what scientists have learned from uncovering ancient artifacts. Create a class "time capsule" for a future generation to find.

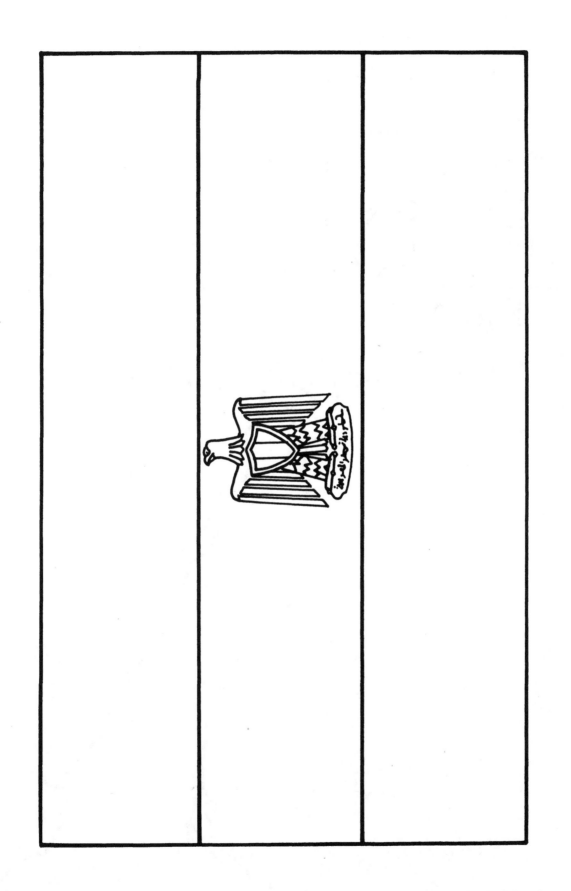

The Flag of Egypt

Egypt

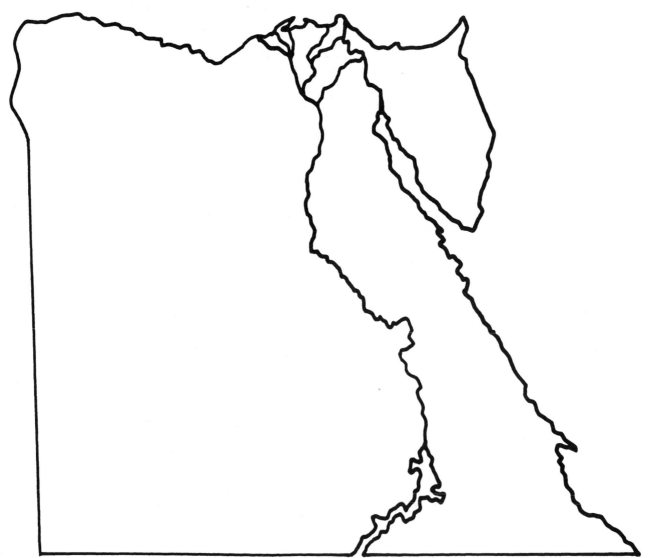

Name _____

Pyramid Word Search

Directions: Have your students find the twelve hidden words and circle each word as they find it. They are written across, down and diagonally. Enlarge this puzzle and use it for the front of a pattern book. Have the students circle the words in the search on the cover and then illustrate the words on the pages of the book.

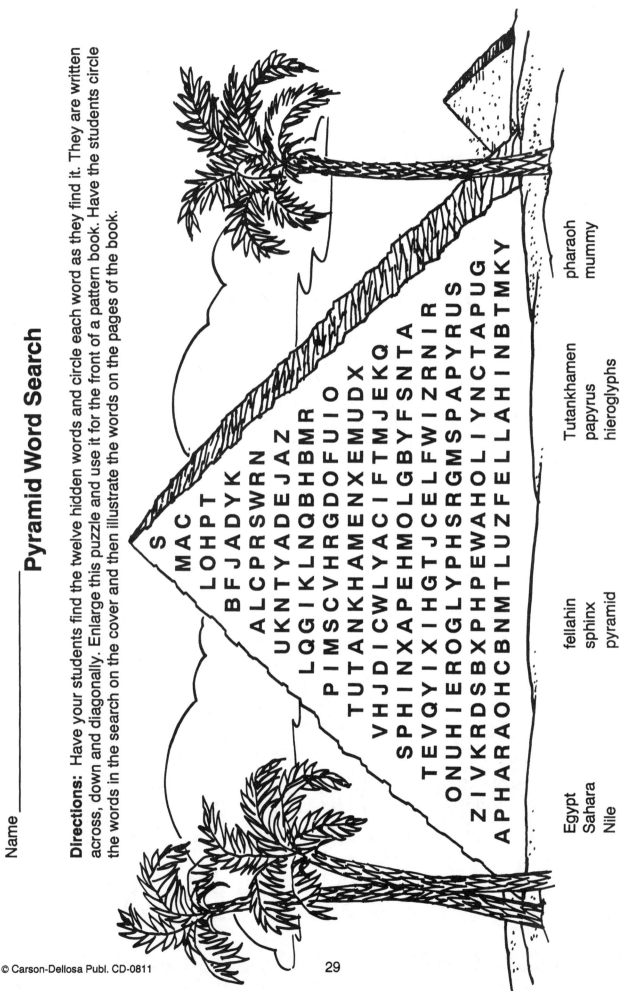

```
S
M A C
L O H P T
B F J A D Y K
A L C P R S W R N
U K N T Y A D E J A Z
L Q G I K L N Q B H B M R
P I M S C V H R G D O F U I O
T U T A N K H A M E N X E M U D X
V H J D I C W L Y A C I F T M J E K Q
S P H I N X A P E H M O L G B Y F S N T A
T E V Q Y I X I H G T J C E L F W I Z R N I R
O N U H I E R O G L Y P H S R G M S P A P Y R U S
Z I V K R D S B X P H P E W A H O L I Y N C T A P U G
A P H A R A O H C B N M T L U Z F E L L A H I N B T M K Y
```

fellahin	Tutankhamen	pharaoh
sphinx	papyrus	mummy
pyramid	hieroglyphs	

Egypt		
Sahara		
Nile		

29

Teacher Resources

Aliki. *Mummies Made in Egypt.* HarperTrophy, 1985.

Climo, Shirley. *The Egyptian Cinderella.* Crowell, 1992.

dePaola, Tomie. *Bill and Pete Go Down the Nile.* Penguin Young Readers Group, 1990.

Donnelly, Judy. *Tut's Mummy: Lost. . . And Found.* Random House, 1988.

Hart, Avery and Mantell, Paul. *Pyramids!: 50 Hands-On Activities to Experience Ancient Egypt.* Ideals Publications, 1997.

Hart, George. *Ancient Egypt.* DK Publishing, Inc., 2004.

Heide, Florence Parry and Gilliland, Judith Heide. *The Day of Ahmed's Secret.* William Morrow & Company, 1995.

Logan, Claudia. *The 5,000-Year-Old Puzzle: Solving a Mystery of Ancient Egypt.* Farr, Straus and Giroux, 2002.

McGraw, Eloise Jarvis. *Golden Goblet.* Penguin Young Readers Group, 1986.

Morley, Jacqueline. *You Wouldn't Want to Be a Pyramid Builder.* Scholastic, 2004.

Morley, Jacqueline and Bergin, Mark. *An Egyptian Pyramid.* Peter Bedrick, 1991.

Pateman, Robert and El-Hamamsy, Salwa. *Egypt.* Marshall Cavendish, Inc., 2003.

Perl, Lila. *Mummies, Tombs and Treasures: Secrets of Ancient Egypt.* Houghton-Mifflin, 1990.

Rius, Maria. *Prehistory to Egypt.* Children's Press Choice, 1988.

Roehrig, Catharine. *Fun with Hieroglyphs.* The Metropolitan Museum of Art and Backpack Books, 2005.

Snyder, Zilpha Keatley. *The Egypt Game.* Random House Children's Books, 1985.

Stolz, Mary. *Zekmet the Stone Carver.* Harcourt, 1988.

Next Stop...Kenya

Area: 224,960 sq. miles
Capital City: Nairobi
Population: 41,070,934
Main Languages: English and Kiswahili
Main Religion: Protestantism
Currency: Kenyan Shilling
Government: Republic
Flag:

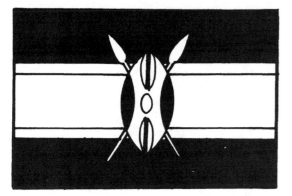

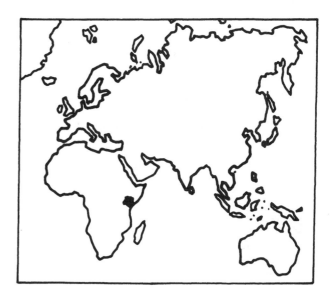

The flag of Kenya has four colors. The top black stripe stands for the Kenyan people, the middle red stripe for their blood and the struggle for independence, and the green stripe for the rich land. The two white stripes represent peace, unity, and the non-African minorities. A Masai war shield is pictured in the center, and it symbolizes the defense of freedom.

For Your Information

Kenya is located on the eastern coast of Africa. Only slightly smaller than Texas, it borders the Indian Ocean and extends into the interior of Africa. Kenya lies exactly on the equator. Most of the country is _____. The majority of the people live in the fertile southern region. Kirinyaga ("mountain of whiteness"), formerly Mount Kenya, is located in the center of Kenya just south of the equator and is an extinct volcano. Kenya has two great lakes, Turkana and Victoria. Lake Victoria, which lies in southwest Kenya, is the second largest freshwater lake in the world.

Most of Kenya's population is black African. They belong to over four different ethnic groups or tribes with different languages, dialects, and customs. Harambee or "pull together" is the nation's motto. This motto was introduced by Jomo Kenyata, Kenya's first prime minister.

Throughout history, Kenya has been an agricultural nation. Farming and ranching are Kenya's main occupations. Droughts and floods have profoundly affected Kenya's economy. Corn is the most widely grown crop and is the primary food in Kenya.

Fascinating Facts

 In Nairobi, Kenya's capital, and other large cities, life-styles are modern and much like others in Western cities. In more remote areas of Kenya, people live in homes made of thatch and dried mud with no modern conveniences.

 The life expectancy in Kenya is only 48 years of age.

 In 1963, Jomo Kenyatta, Kenya's first prime minister, led the country to independence from British rule. "Jamhuri Day," or Kenya's Independence Day, is celebrated on December 12.

 A large railway, which stretches from the coast of Kenya to Uganda, was built by the British in 1903. East African tribes gave it the name Fire Snake.

 Many Kenyans continue the practice of carrying items and packages on their heads. This practice helps to distribute weight, so it is easier to travel from markets and fields by foot.

 A popular sport in Kenya is long-distance running. Two of Kenya's best-known runners are Kipchoge Keino, who won Olympic Gold Medals in 1968 and 1972; and Henry Rono, who held world records in the 1970s.

 Kenya's largest tribe is the Kikuyu. They worship Nagi, a god who they believe lives on Kirinyuga.

 Jewelry and ornaments are signs of respect for a Kikuyu man. The more he wears, the more respect he gains.

 Kenya is famous for its wildlife. The country is home to such animals as elephants, lions, zebras, giraffes, rhinoceroses, warthogs, and other wild game. Safari (Swahili meaning "journey") tours are important to Kenya's tourism industry. Thousands of visitors travel to Kenya each year for game-watching and photography.

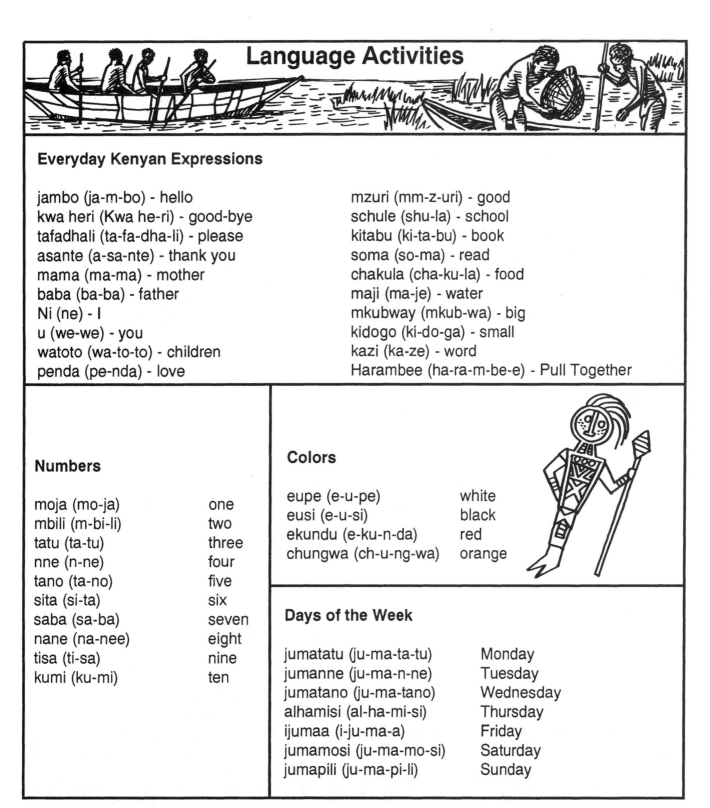

Language Activities

Everyday Kenyan Expressions

jambo (ja-m-bo) - hello
kwa heri (Kwa he-ri) - good-bye
tafadhali (ta-fa-dha-li) - please
asante (a-sa-nte) - thank you
mama (ma-ma) - mother
baba (ba-ba) - father
Ni (ne) - I
u (we-we) - you
watoto (wa-to-to) - children
penda (pe-nda) - love

mzuri (mm-z-uri) - good
schule (shu-la) - school
kitabu (ki-ta-bu) - book
soma (so-ma) - read
chakula (cha-ku-la) - food
maji (ma-je) - water
mkubway (mkub-wa) - big
kidogo (ki-do-ga) - small
kazi (ka-ze) - word
Harambee (ha-ra-m-be-e) - Pull Together

Numbers

moja (mo-ja)	one
mbili (m-bi-li)	two
tatu (ta-tu)	three
nne (n-ne)	four
tano (ta-no)	five
sita (si-ta)	six
saba (sa-ba)	seven
nane (na-nee)	eight
tisa (ti-sa)	nine
kumi (ku-mi)	ten

Colors

eupe (e-u-pe)	white
eusi (e-u-si)	black
ekundu (e-ku-n-da)	red
chungwa (ch-u-ng-wa)	orange

Days of the Week

jumatatu (ju-ma-ta-tu)	Monday
jumanne (ju-ma-n-ne)	Tuesday
jumatano (ju-ma-tano)	Wednesday
alhamisi (al-ha-mi-si)	Thursday
ijumaa (i-ju-ma-a)	Friday
jumamosi (ju-ma-mo-si)	Saturday
jumapili (ju-ma-pi-li)	Sunday

Kenyan Recipes

Tapioca Pudding with Pineapple

Ingredients:
4 cups of water
⅔ cup quick-cooking tapioca
1 cup sugar
½ teaspoon salt
5 cups crushed pineapple
2 tablespoons lemon juice

Directions:
Bring water to a boil in a double boiler. Stir in tapioca, sugar, and salt. Remove from heat. Fold in pineapple and lemon juice. Makes 16 servings.

Irio (a Kikuyan tribe recipe)

Ingredients:
4 cups canned corn
8 potatoes, mashed
1 cup peas

Directions:
Bring corn and peas to a boil. Reduce and simmer until peas are soft. Drain. Mix with mashed potatoes. Add salt to taste.

Safari Animals

Ingredients:
4 cups flour
2 cups salt
2 cups water
food coloring (optional)

(recipe makes enough for 16 animals if you use ½ cup of dough for each)

Directions:
Mix all the ingredients together. Let the students make their animal shapes. Place the shapes on foil and bake at 350° for 20-30 minutes. Cool completely. Let the students paint their animals (acrylic paint works best). You can also mix food coloring into the water before you make the dough. Use these animals with an enlarged copy of the map on page 37 to show where the animals live. Have the students make their own Kenyan safari scenes.

Other Fun Activities

With your class, study the different animals that you might see on a safari. Cut animal pictures out of magazines or make them from clay. This activity could lead to a discussion about endangered and extinct species.

Take a trip to a nearby zoo. Have your children look for animals they might see on a safari. Afterwards, the students can work in cooperative groups to make animal classification posters for farm animals, ocean animals, domestic animals, etc.

Harambee or "pull together" is Kenya's motto. Have your students work with partners or small groups to make up a motto for your classroom. Let the children explain why they chose that motto. Make a banner for the entrance of your classroom with the motto on it. Have your students decorate it.

Learn more about Kenya's largest tribe, the Kikuyu (see page 39). Have the students compare and contrast the Kikuyu life-style with that of people who live in Nairobi and other large cities in Kenya.

The Flag of Kenya

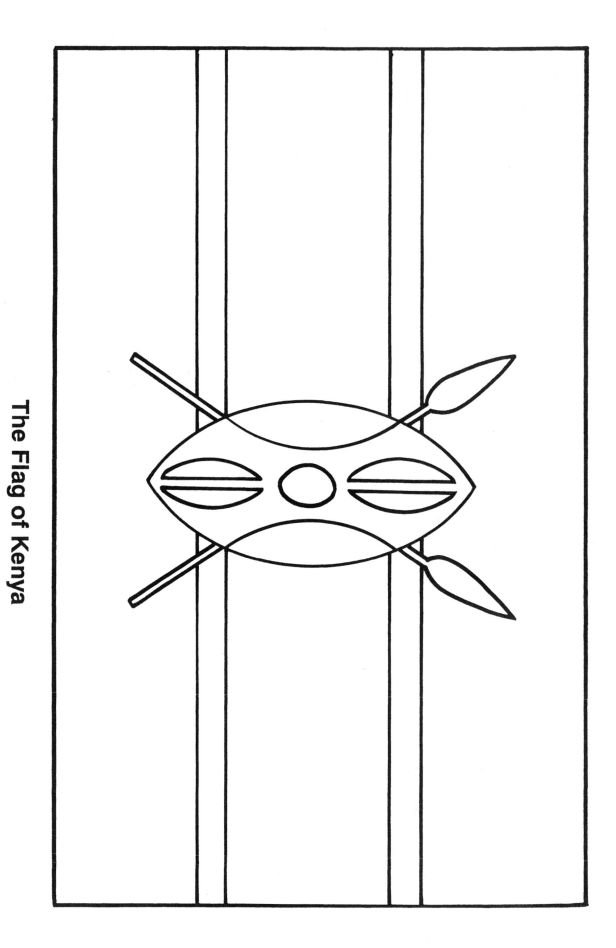

36

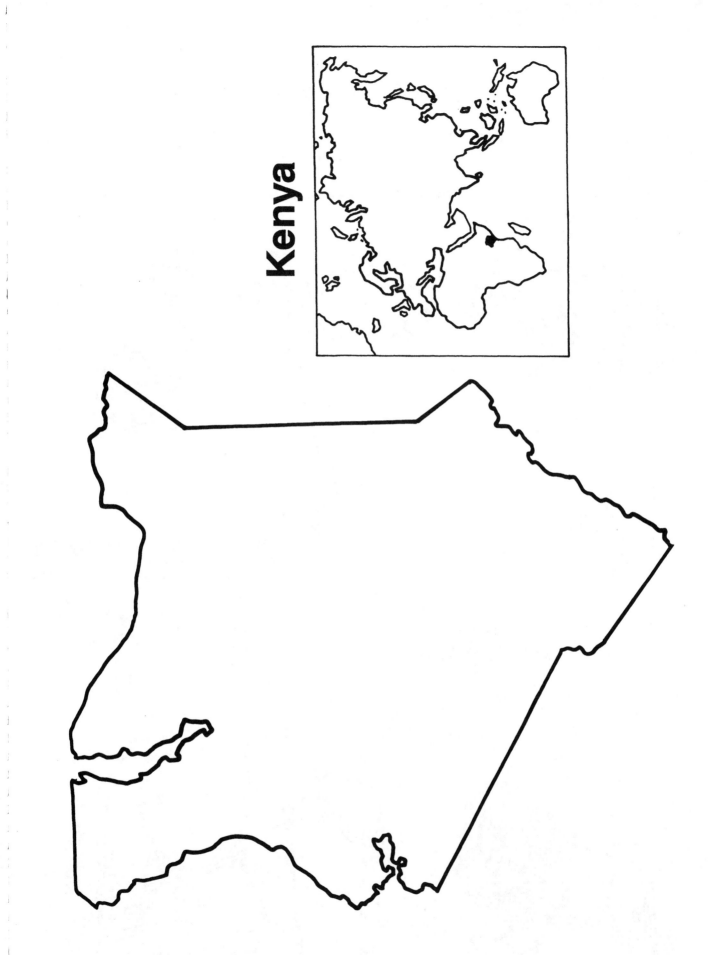

Kenya

Let's Go on Safari!

Directions: Have your students draw a circle around each animal that they might see on a safari through Kenya. Have them cross out the animals that they would not see. Have your students color these animals and cut them out. Glue to tagboard and laminate. Let the kids string them to make a necklace. Glue them to ice cream sticks for puppets and have your students make up a play about endangered animals.

Teacher Resources

Aardema, Verna. *Bringing the Rain to Kapiti Plain*. Dial Books for Young Readers, 1992.

Aardema, Verna. *Rabbit Makes a Monkey of Lion*. Dial Books for Young Readers, 1992.

Bull, Schuyler M. *Through Tsavo: A Story of an East African Savanna*. Soundprints, 1998.

Chamberlin, Mary; Chamberlin, Richard; and Cairns, Julia. *Mama Panya's Pancakes: A Village Tale From Kenya*. Barefoot Books, 2005.

Courlander, Harold. *Cow-Tail Switch and Other West-African Stories*. Henry Holt & Co. Inc, 1987.

Courlander, Harold. *The King's Drum*. Harcourt, Brace and World, 1962.

Feelings, Muriel. *Jambo Means Hello*. Dial Books for Young Readers, 1992.

Feelings, Muriel. *Moja Means One*. Dial Books for Young Readers, 1996.

Haley, Gail E. *A Story, A Story*. Simon & Schuster, 1988.

Heiman, Sarah. *Kenya ABCs: A Book About the People and Places of Kenya*. Picture Window Books, 2002.

King, Bridget A.; Cuthbert, Valerie; Kariuki, Gakuo; and Kioi, Wa Mbugua. *Beneath the Rainbow: A Collection of Children's Stories and Poems from Kenya*. Jacaranda Designs Ltd., 1995.

Lekuton, Joseph Lemasolai. *Facing the Lion: Growing Up Maasai on the African Savanna*. National Geographic Society, 2003.

Sammis, Fran. *Colors of Kenya*. Lerner Publ. Co., 1998.

Winslow, Zachary. *Kenya*. Chelsea House, 1999.

A Visit to Germany

Area: 137,838 sq. miles
Capital City: Berlin
Population: 81,471,834
Main Language: German
Main Religions: Protestantism and
                   Roman Catholicism
Currency: Euro
Government: Federal Republic
Flag:

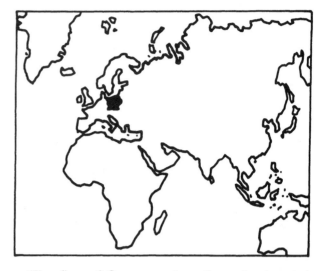

The flag of Germany has three horizontal stripes of black, red, and gold. The colors are associated with the unification of Germany and the colors worn by German soldiers in the early 1800's.

For Your Information

Located in the middle of Europe, Germany is surrouned by nine countries. It has coastlines along the North and Baltic Seas. Hamburg, Germany's largest seaport, is in the northern region. The Black Forest and Bavarian Alps are in the southern region where there are lots of hills.

There are many rivers in Germany. The four main rivers are the Danube, the Elbe, the Odere, and the Rhine. Areas around the Rhine River are best for farming, but most of Germany's soil is poor. Germans have to import most of their food. Germnay's strongest industry is manufacturing, including the production of mother vehicles, machinery, electrical equipment and steel. Germany is the world's third largest producer of cars.

Most Germans live and work in urban areas. Although many Germans have housees, the majority of the people live in apartments. The German language is spoken in many dialects. The two main forms are High German (spoken in central and southern areas), and Low German (spoken in the North). Today, High German is the dialect taught in schools and used by the media.

In 1945, Germany was divided into occupation zones as a result of World War II. In 1949, East and West Germany were created. In 1961, the Berlin Wall was built as a physical separation of the two Germanys. The Berlin Wall was removed in 1989. On October 3, 1990, East and West Germany were reunified.

Fascinating Facts

Many famous dishes were created hundreds of years ago by the Germans to prevent food from spoiling. Sauerkraut was developed to preserve cabbage. Sausages, like bratwurst and frankfurters, were made to preserve meats. Sauerbraten was invented by soaking meat in spices and vinegar.

In Germany, the main meal of the day is usually eaten at lunchtime. It includes meat (particularly pork), vegetables, and a salad. The evening meal usually consists of cold meats, bread, and cheese.

There are over 1,500 types of German sausage. Some of the more popular varieties are weisswurt, birewurst, bratwurst and frankfurters.

Although most Germans wear clothes that are similar to those in America, Germans still wear traditional clothing for festivals, holidays, and other special occasions. Girls wear lacy blouses with brightly-patterned dresses called **dirndls**. **Lederhosen**, leather overall shorts, are worn by boys with alpine hats. Men and women wear these traditional costumes, too.

Germany is famous for its fairy tales by the Grimm Brothers, Jacob and Wilhelm. Some of the fairy tales include *The Frog Prince*, *Goldilocks and the Three Bears*, *Hansel and Gretel*, *Rapunzel*, *Rumplestiltskin*, *The Sleeping Beauty*, and *Snow White and the Seven Dwarfs*.

Manners tend to be formal in Germany. Germans greet friends with a handshake or kisses on both cheeks. When a teacher enters a classroom, students may stand and say "Guten Tag, Frau _____." ("Good day, Mrs. _____.")

Each autumn, Oktoberfest is celebrated in Munich with parades, fancy costumes, and refreshments. The festival originally began in the 1800's to celebrate a royal wedding.

Much of the classical music we enjoy today was composed by German musicians. Johann Sebastian Bach, Ludwig Van Beethoven, Johannes Brahms, and George Frederic Handel are just some of the composers who have given Germany its rich musical history. Today, music remains a popular part of German culture.

Some of the most famous inventions were developed by Germans: the printing press, pocket watches, bicycles, x-ray machines, electric trains, and the Fahrenheit thermometer scale.

There are many castles in Germany, especially along the Rhine River. During the Middle Ages, the castles were built for protection and were often constructed on steep hillsides or on top of rocky cliffs. The castle in Walt Disney's "Sleeping Beauty" was inspired by the Neuschwanstein castle in Southern Germany.

Language Activities

Everyday Expressions

Guten Morgen (gooten morgen) - good morning
Guten Tag (gooten tag) - good day
Auf Wiedersehen (aowf veeder-zayen) - good-bye
der Herr (derr hare) - man
die Frau (die fraow) - woman
der Bub (derr boobe) - boy
das Mädchen (dass maid-khen) - girl
danke schön (danke shurn) - thank you
bitte (bittuh) - please
ja (ya) - yes
nein (nine) - no
der Lehrer (derr layrer) - teacher (male)
die Lehrerin (die layrerin) - teacher (female)
das Märchen - fairy tale
*In German, all nouns are capitalized

Days of the Week

der Montag (derr mun-tag)
der Dienstag (derr deens-tag)
der Mittwoch (derr mitwok)
der Donnerstag (derr donor-stag)
der Freitag (derr fry-tag)
der Samstag (derr sahm-stag)
der Sonntag (derr sown-tag)

*Days are ordered Monday-Sunday.

Numbers

eins (ines)	one
zwei (tsvye)	two
drei (dry)	three
vier (feer)	four
fünf (fewnf)	five
sechs (zex)	six
sieben (seebun)	seven
acht (ahkht)	eight
neun (noyn)	nine
zehn (tsayn)	ten

German Words Used in English

delicatessen
hamburger
kindergarten
pretzel
sauerkraut

Colors

rot (rote) - red
blau (blaow) - blue
gelb (gelp) - yellow
grün (grewn) - green
orange (o-ranje) - orange

rosa (roza) - pink
lila (leela) - purple
schwarz (shvarts) - black
weiss (vyss) - white
braun (brawn) - brown

German Recipes

Potato Pancakes

Ingredients:
5 cups shredded potatoes
1 onion, grated
4 tablespoons flour
4 eggs
¼ teaspoon pepper
¼ teaspoon salt

Directions:
Mix potatoes, onion, and flour. Combine eggs, salt, and pepper in another bowl. Add it to the potato mixture. Heat a small amount of oil in a skillet. Flatten ¼ cup of potato mixture in the skillet and brown on both sides. Remove from heat and place on paper towels. Serve with applesauce. Serves about 12.

Zwetschgenkuchen (German Plum Cake)

Ingredients:
1 pre-made pie shell
3 cups plums (pitted, skinned, and cut in fourths)
¾ cup sugar
2 tablespoons flour
1 teaspoon cinnamon
¼ cup almonds (slivered)
butter

Directions:
Place plums in pie shell. Mix sugar, flour and cinnamon. Sprinkle dry mixture over plums, scatter almonds on top, and cut slivers of butter over the pie. Bake at 375° for 35 minutes or until pastry is golden brown and plums are bubbly.

Host an authentic German meal in your classroom. Since the main meal is usually eaten at lunch-time, your class can prepare a large German meal complete with sauerkraut and other foods native to Germany.

Enjoy some of the music composed by famous German musicians with your class. After listening to classical music, have the students compare and contrast the music with more modern styles like rap, rock-n-roll, beach music, etc.

Research historical castles and their unique designs. The students can make large castles from construction paper and use them as settings for creative writing stories. Collect story books that have castles for settings. During story time, read some of the books you've collected. Do the students think castles would make good homes?

Create a thematic unit around fairy tales written by the Grimm Brothers. Make a story map for each fairy tale. Plot all the characters' movements. Compare and contrast the characters, the settings, and the events. Use a Venn diagram to explain your findings. You can even have a character dress-up day.

Invite a German exchange student to your classroom to give your students a mini-lesson in speaking German. Make posters of the colors, numbers, etc. (see page 42).

The Flag of Germany

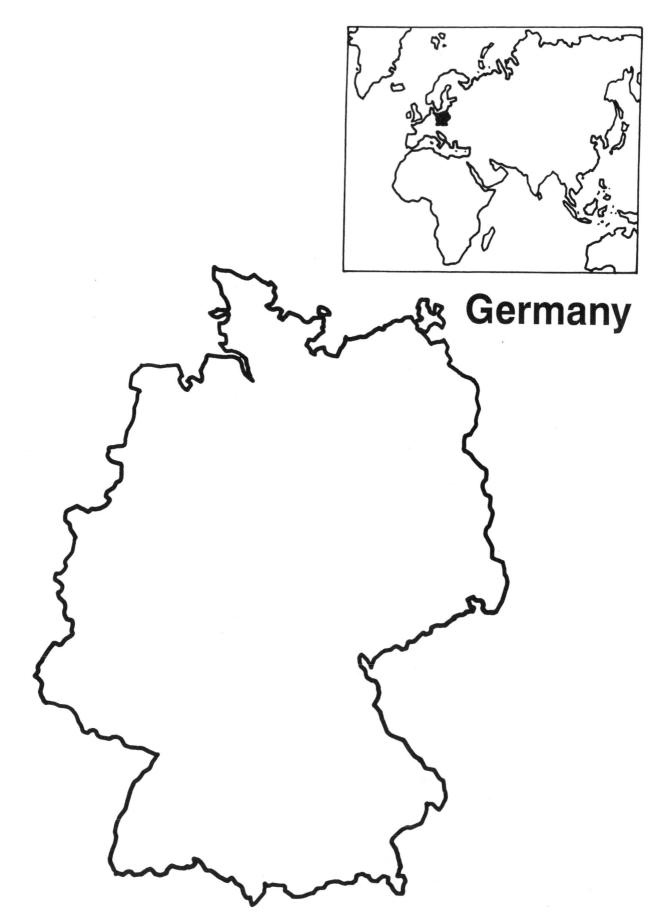

Germany

Decoding

Directions: Can you guess what the girl is saying? Answer the questions using the key below and then fill in the numbered blanks at the bottom of the page.

1. This city is Germany's largest seaport. ___ ___ ___ ___ ___ ___ ___
   1

2. ___ ___ ___ ___ ___ ___ ___ ___ ___ ___ preserves cabbage.
   2

3. ___ ___ ___ ___ ___ ___ ___ ___ ___ ___ ___ is held every fall.
   3

4. In 1989, the ___ ___ ___ ___ ___ ___ Wall was taken down.
   4

5. A traditional dress for girls is called a ___ ___ ___ ___ ___ ___ .
   5

6. These beautiful structures were originally built for protection. ___ ___ ___ ___ ___ ___ ___
   6

7. The forest in southern Germany is called the ___ ___ ___ ___ ___ Forest.
   7

8. The German dialect taught in schools is ___ ___ ___ ___ German.
   8

sauerkraut
High
Black
castles
Hamburg
Oktoberfest
Berlin
dirndl

___ ___ ___ ___ ___ ___ ___ ___
 1   2   3   4   5

___ ___ ___ !
 6   7   8

Teacher Resources

Browning, Robert. *The Pied Piper of Hamelin.* Dover Publications, 1997.

Dahl, Michael S. *Germany.* Capstone Press, 1997.

Davis, Kevin A. *Look What Came From Germany.* Scholastic, 2000.

Gordon, Sharon. *Germany.* Marshall Cavendish, Inc., 2004.

Gray, Susan Heinrichs. *Germany (True Books).* Children's Press, 2003.

Grimm, Jacob and Grimm, Wilhelm. *Grimms' Fairy Tales.* Grosset & Dunlap, 1995.

Haskins, James. *Count Your Way Through Germany.* Carolrhoda Books, 1990.

Heiman, Sarah. *Germany ABCs: A Book About the People and Places of Germany.* Picture Window Books, 2002.

Knorr, Rosanne. *If I Lived in Germany.* Longstreet Press, 1995.

Macaulay, David. *Castle.* The Trumpet Club, 1982.

Parnell, Helga. *Cooking the German Way.* Lerner Publ. Co., 2003.

Plume, Ilse. *The Bremen Town Musicians.* Dragonfly Books, 1998.

Smith, Jeremy. *Fall of the Berlin Wall.* World Almanac Library, 2004.

Van Woerkom, Dorothy. *The Queen Who Couldn't Bake Gingerbread.* Knopf, 1975.

Wright, Nicola; Amos, Janine; Wooley, Kim; and Sansone, Emma. *Getting to Know: Germany and German.* Barron's Educational Services, Inc., 1993.

On to the Netherlands

Area: 15,770 sq. miles
Capital City: Amsterdam
Population: 16,874,007
Main Language: Dutch
Main Religion: Roman Catholicism
Currency: Euro
Government: Constitutional Monarchy
Flag:

The flag of the Netherlands has three horizontal stripes of red, white, and blue. Before 1630, an orange stripe was at the top instead of red to signify the Royal Family of Orange.

For Your Information

   The Netherlands, also referred to as Holland, is located in northwestern Europe. It is surrounded by Germany, Belgium, and the North Sea. The Netherlands is a small country aproximately the size of the states of Maryland and New Jersey combined. Much of the land in the Netherlands is below sea level. In fact, Netherlands means "low lands." The Dutch build dikes (sea walls) to keep water from flooding the cities and the canals which extend inland from the North Sea. Today, over 50 percent of the Netherlands' population live on land that has been recovered from the sea.

   Two major rivers flow through the Netherlands, the Rhin e and the Maas. The rivers are important means of transportation, and the canals connect the rivers to each other and t he North Sea. Rotterdam is the world's biggest seaport.

   Amsterdam is the offical capital, but the official residence of the Queen and the headquarters for the national government is The Hague (known as the City of Peace and Justice), a historic city in the southwestern part of the country.

   Milk, cheese, and flowers are among the Netherland's most famous products. Several thousand different kinds of tulips and other flowers are grown in the country. The flowers and bulbs are flown throughout the world daily.

Fascinating Facts

 Windmills can be found throughout the Netherlands. The Dutch use the windmills as a source of energy for grinding grain and for pumping water. Today, electric motors have replaced most windmills.

 The Netherlands has a monarch, but the country is governed by a parliament. It also has a constitution.

 Most Dutch today wear modern dress. On holidays or special occasions, the Dutch may wear traditional costumes: baggy pants and round hats for the men, and long, colorful dresses with lace caps for the women. The most famous item of Dutch traditional dress is the wooden shoes, or **klompen**. They were developed to protect Dutch feet from the damp ground. The klompen are never worn indoors.

 Ice skating, soccer, bicycle riding, and swimming are popular sports in the Netherlands. When the ice is thick enough, children often ice skate through the canals.

 What we call bowling today originated in the Netherlands from a game called Dutch pins. A ball was aimed at nine pins and the first person to earn a score of 31 was the winner. When the Dutch settled in what is now New York City, they brought the game Dutch pins with them.

 The small town of Delft in the Netherlands has become famous for producing fine, blue and white pottery. Delft pottery is sold in stores throughout the world.

 Celebrating birthdays is very important to the Dutch. Special activities are planned all day long to honor a family member's birthday. These events may include sleeping late and eating with silverware decorated with little bows. The Queen's birthday is the most special of all. It is a national holiday. Girls wear orange ribbons in their hair to honor the Queen's family, the Royal House of Orange.

 On May 4, the Dutch celebrate Memorial Day (a solemn holiday commemorating the end of World War II). At exactly eight o'clock, everyone stops what he or she is doing. Television and radio programs are interrupted, and cars even pull over to the side of the road. Throughout the country, people remember those who died in the war.

 Dairy products are important in the Netherlands. Several well known cheeses are named after the towns where they are produced. For example, Gouda cheese originated in Gouda.

Language Activities

Common Dutch Words

moeder (moo-dher) - mother
vader (v`a-dher) - father
jongen (young-hen) - boy
meisje (melsh-eh) - girl
ja (y`a) - yes
nee (ney) - no
hello (hal-low) - hello
tot ziens (taught-seens) - good-bye

goede nacht (goo-dhe naght) - good night
bliji (blay) - happy
Ik (ick) - I
houvan (howfvan) - love
jou (yow) - you
school (scghool) - school
leraar (heer-áre) - teacher
kuas (kás) - cheese

Numbers

een (ain)- one
twee (tvea) - two
drie (drey) - three
vier (fvear) - four
vijf (fvayf) - five
zes (ses) - six
seven (sal-ven) - seven
acht (aught) - eight
negen (ney-ghen) - nine
tien (teen) - ten

Colors

rood (rude) - red
groen (groon) - green
oranje (or-an-yall) - orange
purperrood (purr-per-rood) - purple
wit (vitt) - white

blauw (blough) - blue
geel (gale) - yellow
anjelier (an-yay-lear) - pink
zwart (zw-art) - black
bruin (broon) - brown

Days of the Week

maandag (mon-d`ag) - Monday
dibsdag (dins-d`ag) - Tuesday
woensdag (woons-d`ag) - Wednesday
donderdag (don-dher-d`ag) - Thursday

vrijdag (fvray-d`ag) - Friday
zaterdag (saa-ter-d`ag) - Saturday
sondag (son-d`ag) - Sunday

Dutch Recipes

Hutspot

Ingredients:
1 pound meat (round steak or chuck roast)
4 potatoes
4 carrots (or mixed vegetables)
1 large onion
salt, pepper, garlic

Directions:
Cut or cube all the ingredients and place in a crock pot with at least ½ cup water. Cook on low heat for about two hours or until the meat is tender. Add water as needed.

Dutch Egg and Cheese

Ingredients:
2 tablespoons of soft margarine
2 green onions, sliced
1 cup cheddar cheese, grated
6 eggs
6 tablespoons of half-and-half
Salt, pepper, and paprika to taste

Directions:
Grease six custard cups or other small serving dishes with margarine. Divide onions and half of the cheese evenly among the cups. Break each egg over a cup (over the cheese). Pour one tablespoon of half-and-half over each egg. Sprinkle each cup with salt, pepper, paprika and the remaining cheese. Bake at 350° for 20-25 minutes. Serves six.

Chocolate Bread

Ingredients:
bread
butter
chocolate chips

Directions:
Spread butter on top of the bread and then sprinkle with chocolate chips. This dessert is especially tasty when heated.

Classroom Activities

There are beautiful flowers in the Netherlands. Introduce your class to different kinds of flowers, including tulips. Have your students plant a variety of bulbs from the Netherlands either at home or at school. You may even want to plant a flower garden or put planters in your classroom window. When the flowers bloom, have a flower show.

After reading *The Silver Skates* (see page 57), take your class on a field trip to an ice skating rink.

Set up a bowling alley in your classroom or in the gym using half gallon plastic jugs and tennis balls. Write questions from desired curriculum area (spelling, math, social studies) on 3" x 5" index cards. Write the answers on the half gallon plastic jugs. Each child can pick a problem from the pile of cards and try to strike down the pin with the correct answer.

Experience the cheeses of the Netherlands. Have a cheese-and juice-tasting party. Compare the foreign cheeses to the domestic ones. You can even have your class research how cheese is made.

In some cities in the Netherlands, there are miniature models of towns that show different scenes of Dutch life. Using small milk cartons, boxes, and other materials, have the children make models of their community or a city in the Netherlands.

The Flag of The Netherlands

The Netherlands

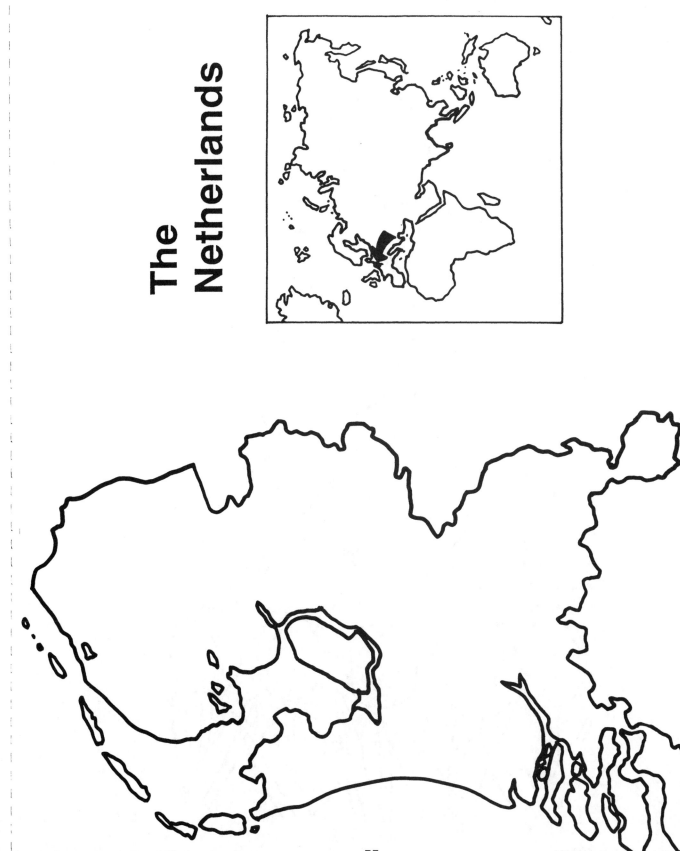

Counting Tulips

Directions: Have the students draw a line to match the tulips with the correct Dutch number word. Have them color the tulips and add grass to make a field. On the back of their papers, have your students write stories about planting a flower garden or receiving an air-mail package of bulbs from the Netherlands.

Drie

Vijf

Een

Vier

Twee

56

Teacher Resources

Borden, Louise. *The Greatest Skating Race: A World War II Story from the Netherlands.* Simon & Schuster, 2004.

Dahl, Michael S. *The Netherlands.* Capstone Press, 1998.

Davis, Kevin A. *Look What Came From the Netherlands!* Scholastic, 2003.

Dodge, Mary Mapes. *Hans Brinker or The Silver Skates.* HaperCollins, 2003.

Heinrichs, Ann; Conroy, Patricia; and Vargus, Nanci R. *The Netherlands (True Books).* Children's Press, 2003.

Hort, Lenny. *The Boy Who Held Back the Sea.* Dial Books, 1987.

Paterson, Katherine and Paterson, John. *Blueberries for the Queen.* HarperCollins, 2004.

Reynolds, Simon and Ngcheong-Lum, Roseline. *Welcome to the Netherlands.* Gareth Stevens Publishing, 2002.

Approaching Saudi Arabia

Area: 839,996 sq. miles
Capital City: Riyadh
Population: 26,417,599
Main Language: Arabic
Main Religion: Islam
Currency: Riyal
Government: Monarchy with Council of Ministers
Flag:

The flag of Saudi Arabia was adopted in 1973. The flag is green, the traditional Muslim color, with a white inscription and sword. The Arabic words state, "There is no god but Allah and Mohammed is his Prophet."

For Your Information

Saudi Arabia is a large Middle Eastern country that occupies most of the Arabian Peninsula in southwestern Asia. There are no permanent rivers or bodies of water in Saudi Arabia. Most of the land is covered by deserts; underneath the desert lies Saudi Arabia's most precious resource, oil.

Saudi Arabia has gained much wealth and power by exporting oil. In fact, Saudi Arabia exports more oil than any other nation in the world. The oil industry supplies nearly all of the nation's income and dominates its economy. Before World War II and the development of Saudi Arabia's oil industry, most of the people lived in rural areas. As the industry developed, large numbers of people moved to cities and towns and enjoyed increased wealth and prosperity. Today, most Saudi Arabians live in urban areas.

There are three major cities in Saudi Arabia. Riyadh is the capital. Jiddah, located next to the holy city of Mecca, is the busiest. Dhahran, situated near the Persian Gulf, is the largest depository of oil in Saudi Arabia.

Fascinating Facts

The lives of most Saudi Arabians are closely governed by Islam, the Muslim religion. They recite prayers five times a day, fast during Ramadan (observance of the first revelation of the Koran made to Mohammed), and must make a pilgrimage (a religious trip) to the Holy City of Mecca at least once.

People in Saudi Arabia still wear traditional clothes in both rural and urban areas. Clothing varies among regions. Generally, men wear long cotton shirts called **kaftan** or **thawbs**. Over the thawb, they wear a **bisht**, or cloak. On their heads, men wear a **kuffiyyah** (skull cap) underneath a **ghoutra** which is a square cloth folded into triangles and draped over the kuffiyyah. It is common to see **asayib** (a head band that holds head gear in place) on both men and women. Women wear a scarf called a **misfa** that covers the head and face except the eyes. They wear **abaayas** (cloaks draped over colorful gowns) that cover them head to toe.

In Saudi Arabia, attending school is required for boys, but not for girls. Boys and girls go to separate schools. Education is free.

The largest desert in Saudi Arabia is called the Rub al Khali, Arabic for "The Empty Quarter," and is located in the south. It is roughly the size of Texas and is almost uninhabited. Some of the windswept sand dunes in the desert reach heights of nearly 1,000 feet. Saudi Arabia receives little rain. Instead, it has sand storms caused by northwesterly winds called **shamals**.

The Saudi Arabian diet consists mostly of dairy products, lamb, rice, and dates. The laws of Islam forbid the eating of pork, smoking, and drinking alcohol.

The **Bedouin** are nomadic herdsman of Saudi Arabia. They travel across the deserts with camels, goats, and sheep in search of water and fertile land for grazing. The Bedouin sleep under goatskin tents that they can take down easily since they move frequently.

The king of Saudi Arabia has total power. He is both the political leader and **imam**, the supreme religious leader. His royal family, consisting of several thousand people, is the most important political group. There is no constitution or voting in Saudi Arabia.

Arabic Alphabet

Alif	ا	Dal	د	Daad	ض	Khif	ك
Ba	ب	Zal	ذ	Tau	ط	Lam	ل
Ta	ت	Ra	ر	Zau	ظ	Mim	م
Sa	ث	Za	ز	Eyn	ع	Noon	ن
Jem	ج	Sín	س	Ghyn	غ	Ha	ه
Ha	ح	Shin	ش	Pha	ف	Vav	و
Kha	خ	Saad	ص	Khaf	ق	Ya	ي

*Arabic is written right to left.

Arabic Numbers

١	٢	٣	٤	٥
1	2	3	4	5

٦	٧	٨	٩	١٠
6	7	8	9	10

Days of the Week

Al-Ithnan - Monday
Al-Toulata - Tuesday
Al-Arbya - Wednesday
Al-Khamees - Thursday
Al-Jumah - Friday
Al-Subth - Saturday
Al-Ahad - Sunday

Everyday Expressions

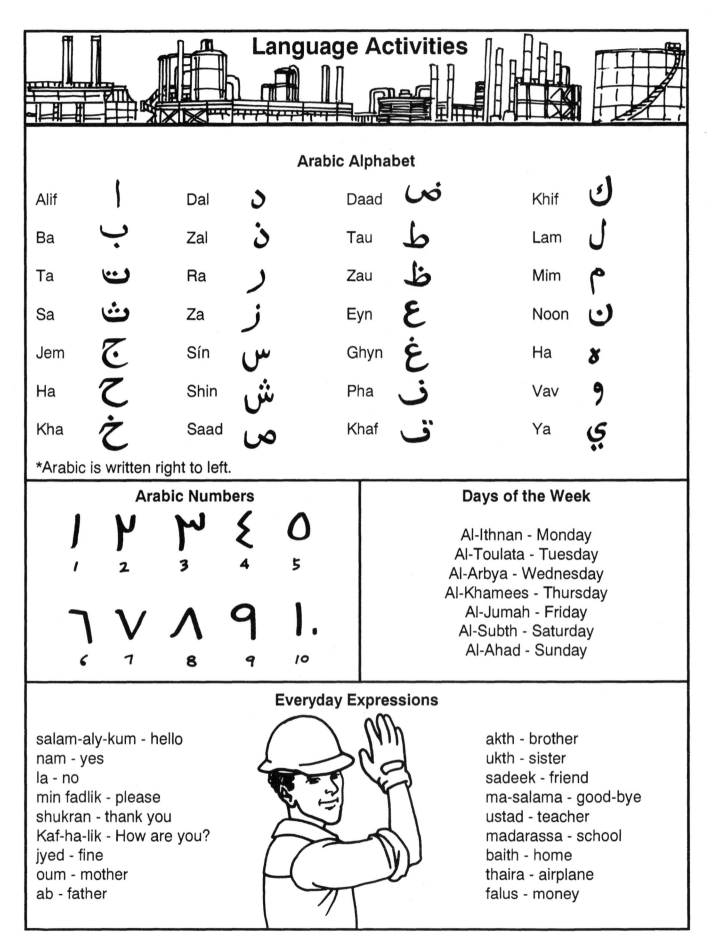

salam-aly-kum - hello
nam - yes
la - no
min fadlik - please
shukran - thank you
Kaf-ha-lik - How are you?
jyed - fine
oum - mother
ab - father

akth - brother
ukth - sister
sadeek - friend
ma-salama - good-bye
ustad - teacher
madarassa - school
baith - home
thaira - airplane
falus - money

Saudi Arabian Recipe

Hummus

Ingredients:
15 oz. can garbanzo beans (save the liquid)
½ cup sesame seeds
1 clove garlic, cut into halves
3 tablespoons lemon juice
1 teaspoon salt
pita bread, cut into wedges

Directions:
Put saved liquid, sesame seeds, and garlic in a blender. Blend on high speed until well mixed. Add beans, lemon juice, and salt. Blend until smooth. Serve as a dip with pita bread.

Classroom Activities

Most people in Saudi Arabia continue to wear traditional dress. Let your students research traditional clothing of other countries. Does the clothing suit the environment? Do the pieces of clothing have any special meaning?

The Rub al Khali Desert in Saudi Arabia covers much of the country. Have your class learn more about the desert environment. Your class can make a large mural depicting the Saudi Arabian desert (plants, animals, shelters, transportation, people, etc.).

Experiment with sand in your classroom. Using large shallow boxes or a water table, your class can make desert scenes. Sprinkle sand mixed with powdered paint over pictures covered with glue on construction paper. A sand center with empty containers can also be a lot of fun.

Make a large camel out of paper for a "fact and opinion" bulletin board. The children can look up facts about camels then share their opinions about camels. You may want to have the children write creative stories on how they believe camels got their humps. Afterwards, read *How the Camel Got His Hump* by Rudyard Kipling (see pg. 66).

All native Saudi Arabians share the Muslim religion. Invite a member of the Muslim religion to your classroom to share with your students his or her religious practices.

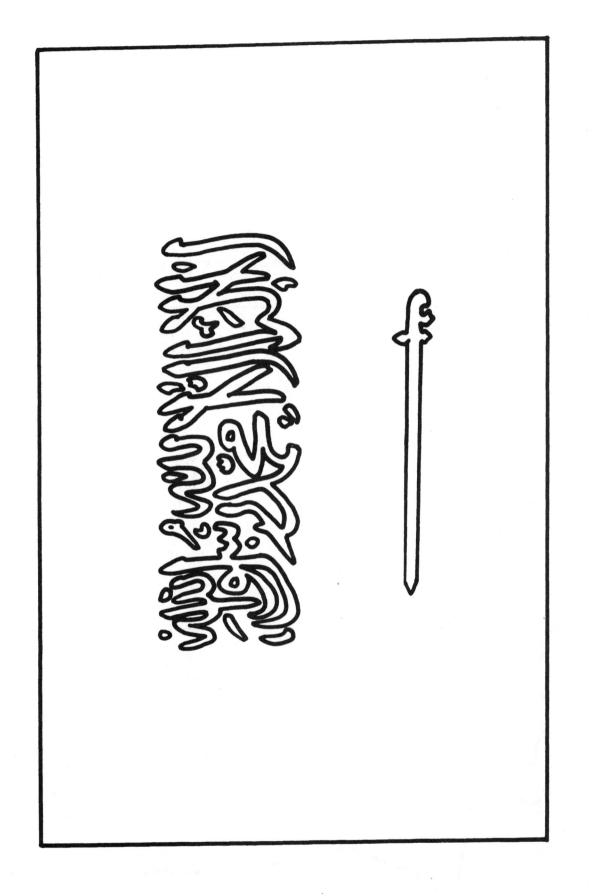

The Flag of Saudi Arabia

Saudi Arabia

64

Name _____

Directions:
- Cut out, color, and glue the patterns to ice cream sticks to make stick puppets.
- Staple paper loops on the back and use them for finger puppets.
- Enlarge and use as covers for books about Saudi Arabia.
- Enlarge, color, glue to tagboard, and laminate. Cut apart pieces and use for a floor puzzle.
- Have your students color the patterns and write their names in Arabic on the front.

Teacher Resources

Broberg, Catherine. *Saudi Arabia in Pictures* (*Visual Geography* Series). Lerner Publ. Co., 2002.

Harper, Robert A. *Saudi Arabia*. Chelsea House Publishers, 2002.

Haskins, Jim. *Count Your Way Through the Arab World*. Carolrhoda Books, 1988.

Heinrichs, Ann and Johnson, Amy J. *Saudi Arabia* (*Enchantment of the World* Series). Scholastic, 1999.

Janin, Hunt and Besheer, Margaret. *Saudi Arabia (Cultures of the World)*. Benchmark Books, 2003.

Kipling, Rudyard. *How the Camel Got His Hump*. Harper, 1985.

Lye, Keith. *Take a Trip to Saudi Arabia*. Franklin Watts, 1984.

Nye, Naomi Shihab. *19 Varieties of Gazelle: Poems of the Middle East*. HarperCollins, 2005.

O'Shea, Maria. *Saudi Arabia*. Gareth Stevens Publishing, 1999.

Landing in China

Area: 3,696,100 sq. miles
Capital City: Beijing
Population: 1,336,718,015
Main Language: Mandarin Chinese
Main Religion: Atheism
Currency: Yuan
Government: Communist State
Flag:

The flag of China was adopted in 1949. There are five yellow stars on a bright red background. The large star stands for the Communist party. The smaller stars represent the four classes of society: workers, peasants, soldiers, and students.

For Your Information

China is located on the continent of Asia and is the third largest country in the world. It is about the size of the continent of Europe. With over one billion people, China is home to one-fifth of the world' population. China's topography is very diverse. There are vast deserts, snowy plains, tropical jungles, fertile farmlands, and subpolar mountainous regions. Mount Everest, the highest mountain in the world, is part of the Himalayan mountain range. Mount Everest straddles the border of Nepal and Tibet; Tibet is politically part of China.

Over two-thirds of Chinese workers are employed in farming. China's main products are rice, wheat, cotton, tobacco, and silk. Rice is a main part of the Chinese diet, and millions of tons of rice must be produced each year to feed the vast population. China is the largest producer of rice, tobacco, and cotton on the world.

China is considered two countries with two governments: The People's Republic of China and The Republic of China. Both mainland China and Taiwan (and three tiny islands in the Formosa Strait) consider themselves the true government of China. China has been divided this way since 1949 when the Chinese Communist Party, led by Mao Zedong, took control of mainland China.

Fascinating Facts

Riding bicycles is a popular means of transportation in China. There are over 130 million bicycles in China and every city has bicycle parks with attendants to look after them.

Some of the common items we use today were invented in China. They include kites, paper money, wheelbarrows, porcelain, and folding umbrellas. American grocery stores carry a variety of foods discovered in China and introduced to the West. Apricots, peaches, oranges, grapefruits, and tea are just a few.

There are several interesting and rare animals that are native to China. The large yak lives in the Himalayan Mountains. Its milk is used to make sour butter which is served in tea. The giant panda lives in the bamboo forests of Sichuan, and wild cranes live near China's marshes. Pandas and cranes have become very rare.

In the northern regions of China, the winter temperatures can fall to 20° below zero.

Stretching about 4,000 miles, the Great Wall of China was built to defend the country from northern attacks. The Great Wall took over 25 years to build, and it is the only man-made structure that can be seen from a spacecraft 200 miles above the earth.

Beijing, the capital of China, hosts the largest public square in the world called Tiananmen Square. At one end of the square is Tiananmen Gate (the Gate of Heavenly Peace). It bears the picture of Mao Zedong, the founder of the Communist People's Republic.

It is a Chinese custom for a child to be considered one year old on the day it is born. A year later, the child is considered to be two-years-old. Celebrations are held for the child a month after birth with banquets, parties, and gifts of red envelopes that contain good luck money. In China, red is the color of happiness and is used for births, weddings, the new year, or any happy occasion.

The Chinese New Year marks the end of winter and the beginning of spring. The Chinese believe it brings good luck for the future. Some of the festivities include parades led by huge dragons, colorful lanterns of all sizes and shapes, fireworks, parties, and red envelopes filled with good luck money.

Favorite sports of Chinese children include soccer, basketball, table tennis, and swimming. They also like to fly kites.

Even though Mandarin Chinese is the official language of China, many Chinese speak other dialects. Also, the official religion of China is atheism because it is a communist country. However, Chinese traditionally practice Buddhism, Taoism, Confucianism and ancestral worship.

Language Activities

The Chinese use characters to represent ideas and objects. There are over 50,000 Chinese characters. The pronunciations given are for Mandarin Chinese.

Chinese Numbers

1	一	yee (ee)
2	二	uhr (arr)
3	三	sahn (san)
4	四	suh (tze)
5	五	woo (wu)
6	六	lyo (leo)
7	七	chee (che)
8	八	bah (ba)
9	九	jo (jieo)
10	十	shur (shr)

Activities:

• Write math problems with these characters. Can the students remember which character means which number?

• Have your students make up their own math problems. Share them with the whole class.

• Play a counting game in Chinese. Count out loud to familiar tunes.

Chinese Recipes

Chopsticks

Try eating a Chinese dish using chopsticks. One stick rests on the crook of your hand between your thumb and index finger. The other stick is supported with the thumb, index and middle fingers. This stick stays on top of the other and will be the one that moves to pick up the food.

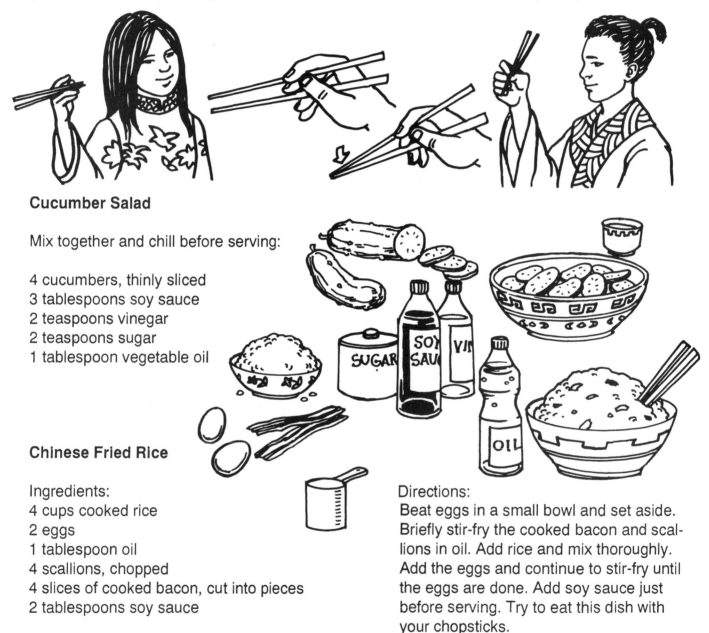

Cucumber Salad

Mix together and chill before serving:

4 cucumbers, thinly sliced
3 tablespoons soy sauce
2 teaspoons vinegar
2 teaspoons sugar
1 tablespoon vegetable oil

Chinese Fried Rice

Ingredients:
4 cups cooked rice
2 eggs
1 tablespoon oil
4 scallions, chopped
4 slices of cooked bacon, cut into pieces
2 tablespoons soy sauce

Directions:
Beat eggs in a small bowl and set aside. Briefly stir-fry the cooked bacon and scallions in oil. Add rice and mix thoroughly. Add the eggs and continue to stir-fry until the eggs are done. Add soy sauce just before serving. Try to eat this dish with your chopsticks.

Chinese Lanterns

The Festival of Lanterns is celebrated on the third day of the Chinese New Year. Make a lantern from colorful paper to hang in your classroom.

Directions:

1. Fold a piece of 12" x 18" construction paper or wallpaper vertically.

2. Cut strips from the folded side stopping 2" from the open edge.

3. Open paper, bend in a circle and then staple.

4. Cut a paper strip and staple as a handle.

More Activities

Make kites or have the students bring them from home. Have a kite festival on the playground.

Celebrate Chinese New Year. Make colorful lanterns (see directions above) and have a parade with paintings of dragons and streamers. Make red envelopes from construction paper and fill them with good luck wishes for friends and family.

Invite someone who knows Tai Chi Chuan (a form of meditation) to your classroom. He or she can teach your students some basic moves and then give a demonstration.

Working in cooperative groups, have the students gather information on the different regions and territories of China. Each group can share with the class what they learned about the people, geography, culture, etc.

The Flag of China

China

Chinese Lantern Word Search

Directions: Have your students find the twelve hidden words and circle the words as they find them. They are written across, down and diagonally. You can also enlarge this lantern and give a copy to each child for coloring. Hang them from the ceiling for decoration.

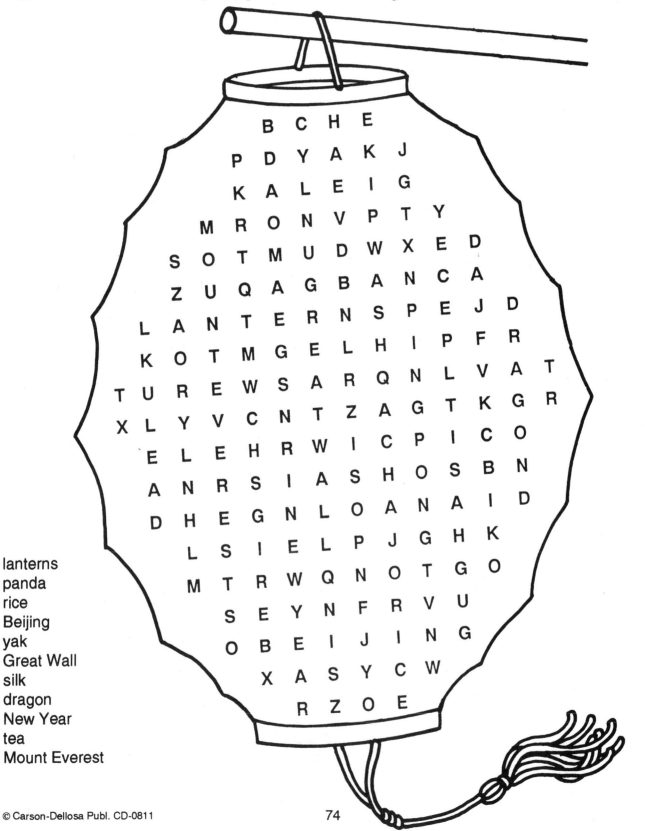

lanterns
panda
rice
Beijing
yak
Great Wall
silk
dragon
New Year
tea
Mount Everest

74

Teacher Resources

Andersen, Hans Christian. *The Nightingale*. Candlewick, 2002.

Dramer, Kim. *People's Republic of China* (*Enchantment of the World* Series). Children's Press, 1999.

Fang, Linda. *The Ch'i-lin Purse: A Collection of Ancient Chinese Stories*. Farrar, Straus and Giroux. 1998.

Flack, Marjorie. *The Story About Ping*. Viking, 1977.

Harvey, Miles. *Look What Came From China!* Franklin Watts, 1999.

Haskins, Jim. *Count Your Way Through China*. Carolrhoda Books, 1988.

Heinrichs, Ann. *China* (*True Books*). Children's Press, 1997.

Kalman, Bobbie. *China: The Culture*. Crabtree Publishing Co., 2000.

Lobel, Arnold. *Ming Lo Moves the Mountain*. HarperTrophy, 1993.

Mosel, Arlene. *Tikki Tikki Tembo*. Henry Holt & Co., 1968.

Pittman, Helena Clare. *A Grain of Rice*. Yearling, 1995.

Simonds, Nina and Swartz, Leslie. *Moonbeams, Dumplings and Dragon Boats: A Treasury of Chinese Holiday Tales, Activities and Recipes*. Gulliver Books, 2002.

So, Sungwan. *C Is for China*. Silver Press, 1997.

Steele, Philip. *Journey Through China*. Troll Communications, 1991.

Yep, Laurence. *The Dragon Prince: A Chinese Beauty and the Beast Tale*. HarperTrophy, 1999.

Yolen, Jane. *The Emperor and the Kite*. Putnam, 1998.

A Visit to Japan

Area: 145,856 sq. miles
Capital City: Tokyo
Population: 126,475,664
Main Language: Japanese
Main Religions: Buddhism and Shintoism
Currency: Yen
Government: Constitutional Monarchy with a
Parliamentary Government

Flag:

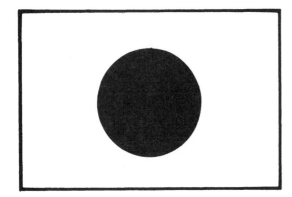

The Japanese flag has a red circle, or "rising sun" on a white background. The red sun stands for warmth, brightness, and sincerity, while the white symbolizes purity and integrity. The flag was adopted in 1854.

For Your Information

The Japanese call their country **Nippon**, which means "land of the rising sun." Japan is located in the Pacific Ocean off the coast of mainland China. Japan is slighly smaller than California, and consists of four large islands and thousands of smaller ones. The largest island is Honshu. Fuji-san, better known to Westerners are Mount Fuji, is the highest mountain in Japan. It is located on the Island of Honshu to the southwest of Tokyo.

Japan is one of the most densely populated countries in the world. Most people live on the narrow coastal plains and over three-fourths of the population is crowdedd into towns and cities.

Japan produces over eight million cars each year and is the world's leading automobile manufacturing country. Japan is also a world leader in the production of electronic equipment. Some of the larger Japanese corporations guarantee their workers lifetime employment. Rice is the most important crop in Japan. Farmers grow crops on terraced fields since the land is so mountainous.

Fascinating Facts

 Children go to school in Japan five and one-half days a week. The school year begins in April and ends in March of the following year. Their summer vacation is from late July to mid August. School can be very difficult in Japan and many children go to **juku**, a cram school held in the evening that helps students keep up with their regular school work.

 Most Japanese today wear western-styled clothing. During holidays, festivals, and other special occasions they may wear traditional robes called **kimonos**. The patterns on kimonos change with the seasons to reflect the seasonal changes in nature. An **obi**, a large decorative sash, is tied around the waist of the kimono.

 Girls in Japan look forward to March 3 when the Doll's Festival, or Peach Festival, is celebrated. Girls display special dolls that may have been in their families for generations.

 The boys of Japan hold a festival on May 5 known as Children's Day. The boys hang carp banners over their homes. The carp, a fish that swims upstream, is considered to be a strong and brave fish.

 The most common food in the Japanese diet is rice. It is served at almost every meal. In fact, the Japanese word for breakfast means "first rice." Fish is the main source of protein for the Japanese and a popular dish is **sushi**, rice and raw fish wrapped in seaweed. **O-cha** is also popular. It is a weak, green tea served without sugar or milk.

 Ikebana, the art of flower arranging, is taught and practiced throughout Japan. In addition to flower arranging, other art forms are: the cultivation of miniature **bonsai** trees, the writing of **haiku** and **tanka** poetry, and **origami**, the art of paper folding.

 Much of Japanese architecture is in the traditional Shinto and Buddhist style of architecture with tile roofs that extend upwards. This type of architecture emphasizes harmony between the buildings and the nature around them.

 Most homes in Japan are small since the land is expensive and crowded. The homes are simply furnished and many have straw mats on the floor called **tatami**. Bedding is called a **futon**. The futons can be folded and put away in the daytime. While nearly every household has a telephone, washing machine, and a television, most Japanese homes have a traditional nook called a **tokonoma**. Beautiful flower arrangements might be found in the tokonoma as well as decorative scrolls.

 The Japanese have strong family ties and deep respect for authority. In Japan, it is polite to greet one another by bowing.

Language Activities

Everyday Japanese Words

ohayo gozaimasu (oh-hi-yo go-zai-mus) -good morning
konnichi wa (co-hnee-chee wah) - good afternoon
komban wa (com-ban wah) - good evening
sayonara (sigh-oh-nah-rah) - good-bye
doozo (dough-zo) - please
arigato (ah-ree-gah-toe) - thank you
haha (ha-ha) - mother
chichi (chee-chee) - father
onna noko (on-nah-no-koh) - girl
otokonoko (o-to-co-no-co) - boy

Music

Number Song
(Sung to "Three Blind Mice")

Ichi, ni, san	One, two, three
Ichi, ni san	One, two, three
Shi, go, roku	Four, five, six
Shi, go, roku	Four, five, six
Shichi, hachi, ku, ju	Seven, eight, nine, ten
Shichi, hachi, ku, ju	Seven, eight, nine, ten
Ichi, ni, san	One, two, three
Ichi, ni, san	One, two, three

Jellied Plums

Ingredients:
8 large grapes or small plums (double recipe for larger number of students)
1 ½ cups of fruit juice
2 ½ envelopes unflavored gelatin
¼ cup warm water
2 ½ tablespoons sugar

Directions:
Put grapes or plums into boiling water for ten seconds. Remove and put into ice water until cool. Remove skins. In a large pot, dissolve gelatin in warm water. Add fruit juice and sugar. Heat until dissolved. Divide gelatin mixture between 8 plastic cups. Add one piece of fruit to each cup. Chill until firm.

Onigiri (Rice Balls)

Ingredients:
Sticky rice
Tuna fish
Water
Spinach

Directions:
Cook rice in a covered pot on the stove or in an electric rice cooker. Steam until soft and sticky. Cool slightly. Give each child a small handful of rice, a paper towel, and a bowl of water. Wet hands to keep the rice from sticking. Make balls out of the rice. Put a teaspoon of tuna inside. Traditional onigiri can be wrapped in seaweed, but you can use spinach as a substitute.

Classroom Activities

The United States imports many items that are made in Japan. Have your students make a list of items found in their homes that were made in Japan. Your class can create a collage of common Japanese products by using old magazines and advertisements in newspapers.

Many Japanese collect dolls and their collections are often displayed. Celebrate this custom by having a "Doll Day." Both the girls and the boys can bring to school special dolls, stuffed animals, and toys that were handed down from their parents or other family members. The dolls are often displayed for everyone to admire.

Make colorful Japanese carp to hang in your classroom. Enlarge and cut out fish patterns (see page 83) from construction paper. Using a paint brush and a mixture of half glue and half water, gently "paint" over the tissue paper so that there are no dry spots. When the carp dry, they can be hung from the ceiling or attached to a stick and waved.

Invite someone of Japanese heritage to your classroom to share with the children the different pieces of Japanese traditional dress. You may even want to have a traditional Japanese tea ceremony.

Create your own tokonoma (see page 77). Your class can paint flowers using tempera paint, water colors, or even tissue paper to make small buds. Make pretty vases out of cartons, cans, etc.

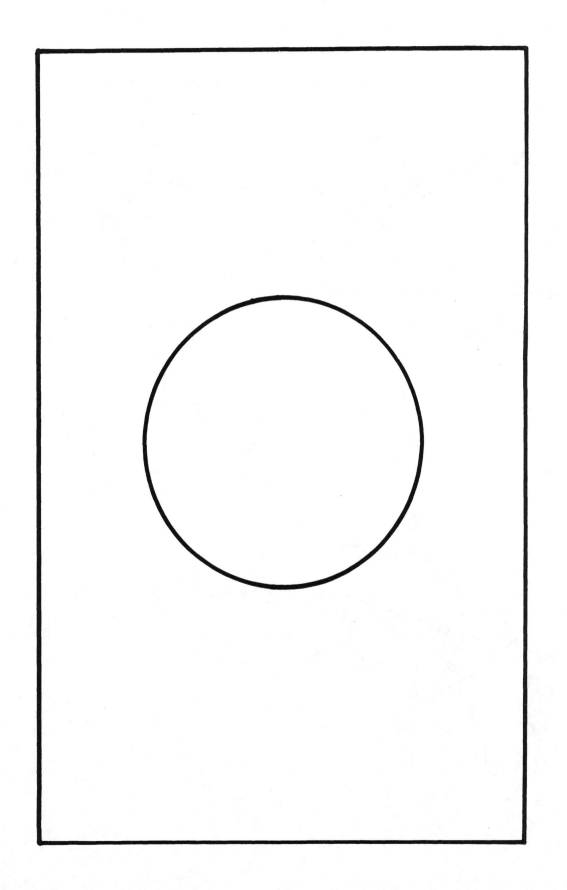

The Flag of Japan

81

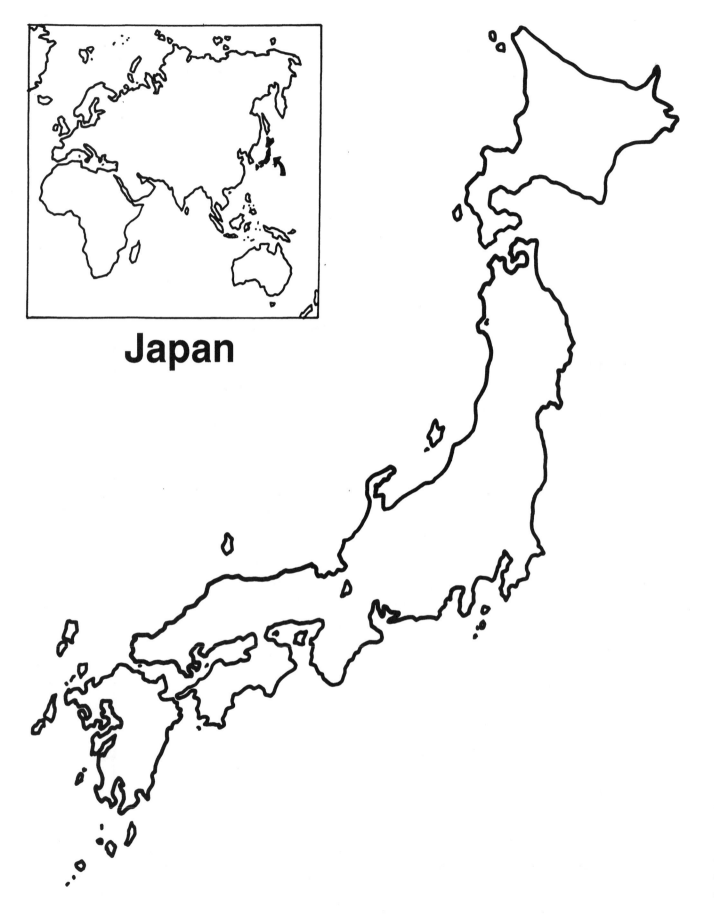

Japan

82

Name _____

Japanese Carp

Directions: Have your students color appropriately. Also, you can cut out, color, glue to tagboard, and laminate. Have the children string them together for a necklace.

aka (red)   ao (blue)   kiiro (yellow)   midori (green)

orenji (orange)   murasaki (purple) chairo (brown)   kuro (black)   shiro (white)

Teacher Resources

Buck, Pearl S. *The Big Wave*. HarperTrophy, 1986.

Coatsworth, Elizabeth. *The Cat Who Went to Heaven*. Aladdin Books, 1990.

Coerr, Eleanor. *Mieko and the Fifth Treasure*. Puffin Books, 2003.

Coerr, Eleanor. *Sadako and the Thousand Paper Cranes*. Puffin Books, 1999.

Freidman, I. R. *How My Parents Learned to Eat*. Houghton Miffllin, 1987.

Haskins, Jim. *Count Your Way Through Japan*. Lerner Publ. Co., 1988.

Heinrichs, Ann. *Japan*. Children's Press, 1997.

Kalman, Bobbie. *Japan, The People*. Crabtree Publishing Co., 2000.

Kimmel, Eric A. *Sword of the Samurai: Adventure Stories from Japan*. HarperCollins, 2000.

Kimmel, Eric A. *Three Samurai Cats: A Story from Japan*. Holiday House, Inc., 2004.

McDermott, Gerald. *The Stonecutter: A Japanese Folk Tale*. Puffin Books, 1978.

Mosel, Arlene. *The Funny Little Woman*. Puffin, 1993.

Paterson, Katherine. *Of Nightingales That Weep*. HarperCollins Children's Books, 1989.

Paterson, Katherine. *The Sign of the Chrysanthemum*. HarperCollins Children's Books, 1988.

Roberson, John, R. *Japan from Shogun to Sony*. Macmillan, 1985.

Roberts, Jeremy. *Japanese Mythology A to Z*. Facts on File, 2003.

Say, A. *Tree of Cranes*. Houghton Mifflin, 1991.

Yashima, Taro. *Crow Boy*. Puffin, 1976.

Arriving in Australia

Area: 2,966,200 sq. miles
Capital City: Canberra
Population: 21,766,711
Main Language(s): English
Main Religion(s): Roman Catholicism, Anglicanism,
                 and Protestantism
Currency: Australian Dollar
Goverment: Democracy
Flag:

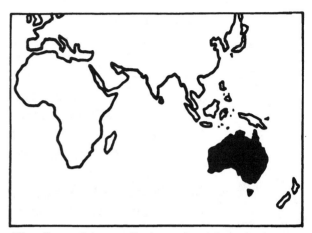

The flag of Australia is red, white, and blue. The British Union flag is at the top, representing the link with Great Britain. The five stars on the right represent the Southern Cross constellatin. The larger star is known as the Commonwealth Star. Five of the six stars have seven points. THe seven points stand for Australia's six states and one territory.

For Your Information

In 1770, a British explorer, James Cook, became the first European to sight and explore a new "island continent." Cook anmed the land New South Wales. The name was later changed to Australia, derived from the Latin word, ***australis***, meaning southern. Australia is the only country that is also a continent. Australia is entirely in the southern hemisphere and is often referred to as being "down under."

Australia is one of the world's most urban countries. Most of the people live in the southeastern region where the two largest cities, Sydney and Melbourne, are located. The interior, or outback of Australia is mostly desert and has very few settlements. The outback has open countryside (bush) and most of the roads are not paved.

For thousands of years, only the native people called Aborigines lived in Australia. After the discovery of Australia, Great Britain began sending prisoners there to work and live in camps. Great Britain stopped this practice in the 19th century. Today, most Australians are of British or Irish ancestry.

Like Great Britain, Australia is a constitutional monarchy. Queen Elizabeth II, the British Monarch, is also the head of state of Australia, but the Queen has little power. Instead, Australia has its own federal government and is divided into six states that have their own governments.

Fascinating Facts

Australia is home to many unique and interesting animals. A lot of the mammals in Australia are marsupials. Marsupials are mammals that carry their under-developed young in a pouch on their stomach after birth. There are over 120 species of marsupials in Australia. Kangaroos, koalas, wombats, and wallabies are just a few. There is an explanation for why Australia's animals are unlike any others. The world used to be one landmass and about 200 million years ago, Australia broke away from the mainland. This separation caused the animals of Australia to develop unlike any other animals on the main landmass.

The platypus, which lives only in Australia, is one of two mammals that hatches its young from eggs. The platypus has a bill and webbed feet like a duck.

Australians love outdoor living and outdoor sports. Many people enjoy swimming, surfing, skin diving, and boating. Tennis and golf are also popular. The most popular team sports in Australia are cricket, rugby, Australian rules football, and soccer.

In some remote areas of Australia, children can get an education without ever going to school. Students belong to School of the Air (correspondence school) and communicate with the teachers by using two-way radios. The teachers are stationed at broadcasting centers. Assignments are received and turned in by mail.

Near the center of the Outback is a huge, red rock that has been shaped by strong winds. It is called Uluru (or Ayers Rock). There are many small caves in Uluru, and the walls are covered with paintings made by the Aborigines many years ago.

Although the climate differs from one part of the country to another, Australia generally has a warm and dry climate. Australia lies south of the equator so the seasons are opposite those in the Northern Hemisphere. While countries in the Northern Hemisphere are having winter, Australia is experiencing summer.

Most people in Australia live in single-story homes, each with its own yard and garden. In fact, apartment buildings are rare in Australia. On the other hand, some of the Aborigines still live like their ancestors. Most Aborigines live on reservations set up by the government, or they live in the cities.

The Great Barrier Reef is the largest coral reef in the world, and is one of Australia's most popular tourist attractions. The reef extends along Australia's northeast coast and is home to over 400 different species of coral and thousands of different types of sea life. The waters around The Great Barrier Reef are warm year-round and attract many skin divers.

Language Activities

Everyday Expressions

g'day - good day
mate - friend
cobber - friend or coworker
ta - good-bye
Oz - Australia
tea - dinner
onkey-dorey - good
fair dinkum - genuine, the honest truth
dinky-do - the real thing
barbie - a barbecue
tucker - food
sandshoes - sneakers
lollies - candy
lolly water - soft drinks
biscuits - crackers
boomer - big kangaroo
to smoodge - to kiss
cozzie - bathing suit
mum - mother
beaut - great

Waltzing Matilda
(A Popular Australian Song)

"Waltzing Matilda" is the story of a hike taken by a swagman (wanderer) and his matilda (bedroll). He goes camping by a billabong (pond) and waits for his billy (pail used for heating water) to boil underneath a coolibah (type of gum tree). The swagman captures a jumbuck (sheep) in his tuckerbag (travelling bag). You can find the music to this song on Multicultural Rhythm Sticks by Georgiana Stewart (published by Kimbo Educational Records, 1992).

Once a jolly swagman camped by a billabong,
Under the shade of a coolibah tree;
And he sang as he watched and waited till his billy
    boiled,
"You'll come a-waltzing Matilda with me!"

Waltzing Matilda, Waltzing Matilda,
You'll come a-waltzing Matilda with me,
And he sang as he watched and waited while the
    billy boiled.
"You'll come a-waltzing Matilda with me!"

Down came a jumbuck to drink at that billabong
Up jumped the swagman and grabbed him with
    glee,
And he shoved that jumbuck into his tuckerbag,
"You'll come a-waltzing Matilda with me!"

Waltzing Matilda, Waltzing Matilda,
You'll come a-waltzing Matilda with me,
And he sang as he watched and waited while the
    billy boiled.
"You'll come a-waltzing Matilda with me!"

*Permission granted for use of above lyrics by Kimbo Educational Records, Long Beach, NJ.

Australian Recipes

Damper Bread

Ingredients:
6 cups self-rising flour
3 teaspoons salt
¾ cup margarine
1 cup milk
1 cup water

Directions:
Mix flour and salt in a bowl. Cut in margarine and mix well. Add water and milk. Mix until well blended. Set aside in a bowl covered with a damp cloth and let rise for 35-40 minutes. Put on a floured board and knead lightly. Shape into two round loaves and put on a greased cookie sheet. Before baking, cut an "x" on the top of the loaves about ½" deep. Brush the tops of loaves with milk. Bake for ten minutes in a 400° oven. Reduce head to 350° for 15 minutes. Let cool and enjoy.

Australian Meat Pie

Ingredients:
2 pounds ground beef
1 cup ketchup
1 cup chopped onion
1 teaspoon salt
1 cup milk
⅔ cup bread crumbs
1 teaspoon oregano
½ teaspoon pepper
2 tablespoons Worcestershire sauce
2 cups shredded cheddar cheese
2 eight-inch pie shells

Directions:
Combine first eight ingredients. Mix well. Place in pie shells and bake at 350° for about 45 minutes. Mix together Worcestershire sauce and cheese. Spread on top. Bake for about 10 more minutes or until cheese is melted.

Classroom Activities

Create a large bulletin board depicting Australia's animals (kangaroos, platypuses, kookaburras, wallabies, etc.). After learning more about these animals, the students can create models of them using construction paper or clay. For creative dramatics, have your class take turns acting like the different animals.

Transfer the expressions from page 87 to large chart paper. Have the students write sentences using the Australian expressions. Can you think of any words or expressions that are unique to your state or region?

Try having a School of the Air in your classroom. Create toy, two-way radios by attaching a long string from the bottom of one tin can to another. Have students give and receive assignments through the mock telephones.

Explore the Great Barrier Reef. Check out library books that the children can use for reference. Have your class make dioramas of the reef using shoe boxes. On the inside of the box, the students can create a reef scene that shows the beautiful fish and coral. For an underwater effect, cover the top of the box with blue colored-plastic wrap.

Australians enjoy cricket. Research the rules of the game and try playing the sport during outside time. Is cricket similar to any American games?

The Flag of Australia

Australia

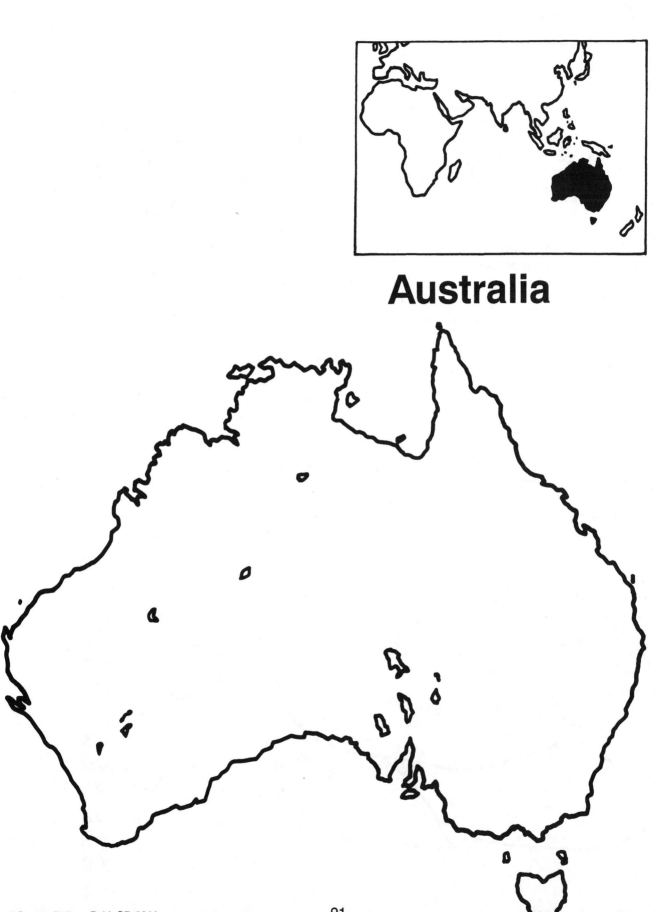

Name _____

Australia is a small country.

Aborigines are native Australians.

Most people in Australia live in the outback.

James Cook was the first European to explore Australia.

The Great Barrier Reef is the largest coral reef in the world.

Marsupials are common in Australia.

Ice hockey is the national sport of Australia.

Ayers Rock is located in the outback.

Teacher Resources

Arnold, Caroline. *Australian Animals*. HarperCollins, 2000.

Banting, Erin. *Australia: The People*. Crabtree Publishing Co., 2002.

Base, Graeme. *My Grandma Lived in Gooligulch*. Harry N. Abrams, 1990.

Davis, Kevin. *Look What Came From Australia*. Franklin Watts, 2000.

Fowler, Allan. *Australia (Rookie Read-About Geography)*. Children's Press, 2001.

Fox, Mem. *Koala Lou*. Voyager Books, 1994.

Fox, Mem. *Possum Magic*. Voyager Books, 1991.

Germein, Katrina. *Big Rain Coming*. Clarion Books, 2000.

Heiman, Sarah. *Australia ABCs: A Book About the People and Places of Australia*. Picture Window Books, 2002.

Olawsky, Lynn Ainsworth. *Colors of Australia*. Carolrhoda Books, 1997.

Petersen, David. *Australia (True Books)*. Children's Press, 1998.

Sayre, April Pulley. *G'Day Australia! (Our Amazing Continents)*. Millbrook Press, 2003.

Trinca, Rod and Argent, Kerry. *One Wooly Wombat*. Kane/Miller Book Publishers, 1991.

Wolkstein, Diane. *Sun Mother Wakes the World: An Australian Creation Story*. HarperCollins, 2004.

Traveling on to Canada

Area: 3,849,000 sq. miles
Capital City: Ottawa
Population: 34,030,589
Main Languages: English and French
Main Religions: Roman Catholicism and
Protestantism
Currency: Canadian Dollar
Government: Federal Parliamentary Democracy
with a Constitutional Monarchy

Flag:

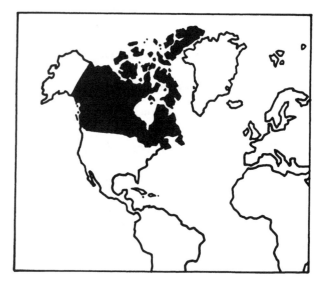

The flag of Canada has red and white
vertical stripes with a red maple leaf in
the center. The maple leaf is a Canadian
symbol because of the abundance of
maple trees.

For Your Information

Canada is the second largest country in the world. It is divided into ten provinces. From the
east, they are as follows: Newfoundland and Labrador, Prince Edward Island, Nova Scotia, New
Brunswick, Quebec, Manitoba, Saskatchewan, Alberta, Ontario, and British Columbia. Canada's
three territories are Yukon, Nunavut, and Northwest Territories. The provinces and territories are
all very different and beautiful. With snowcapped mountains, rolling prairies, and modern cities,
Canada has a rich and diverse land as well as people.

Canada has two official languages, English and French. Both languages are used by the
federal government and are spoken throughout Canada. Each province is given a choice about
which language it will use. Most of the French Canadians live in the province of Quebec, and
they strive to keep the language and customs of their ancestors.

Although most Canadians are of European descent, primarily from Great Britain and France,
some are Native Canadians and Inuits. Inuit means "the people" in the Inuktitut language. Most
Inuits today live in settlements, but they also inhabit most of the thinly populated Arctic lands.

Canada's wealth comes from manufacturing and its abundance of natural resources which
include uranium, zinc, gold, and oil. Canada is also one of the world's largest producers of wheat
and pulpwood.

Fascinating Facts

Some of the Canadian police ride horses instead of using cars. They are called the Royal Canadian Mounted Police, or Mounties. The Mounties were founded in 1873.

Although no one has counted them all, it is believed that Canada has almost a million lakes, more than any other country. There is a lake in Manitoba called Lake Pekwachnamaykoskwaskwaypinwanik.

Bears, moose, deer and other northern animals make themselves at home in the Canadian forests. Black bears, which live all over Canada, are protected by law.

The blue whale, the largest living animal, lives in the Arctic Ocean. Other animals that live in the arctic region of Canada are narwhals, seals, polar bears and walruses.

In the far northern region of Canada, the sun scarcely sets for most of the summer. This is known as the "midnight sun." In June, the sun may not set at all. When it is time to go to bed, the sun may still be shinning. In the winter, it is dark most of the time.

More dinosaur bones have been found in Alberta, Canada than any other place in the world.

Joe Shuster, one of the creators of the famous action comic strip "Superman," grew up in Canada. He met Jerry Siegel as a teenager, and together they developed the character of Superman in the early 1930s. "Superman" was the comic business's first real hit and has since become a regular part of pop culture.

The setting of the popular children's story *Anne of Green Gables* was on Prince Edward Island, Canada.

Niagra Falls, a famous tourist spot, is on the border of Canada and the United States.

Ice hockey is Canada's most popular sport. Most parks have an ice rink, and children begin to play in amateur leagues when they are seven years old.

Lacrosse is the national sport of Canada. The sport was first played by the Iroquois Indians. Their original game was meant to be played with hundreds of people.

Like Australia, Canada recognizes the Queen of Great Britain as its head of state. Great Britain ruled Canada until 1867. Today, Canada is an independent, self-governing nation.

Language Activities

Everyday French Expressions

bonjour (bon-zhoor)	hello
au revoir (or-re-vwar)	good-bye
l' anniversaire (la-nee-vers-air)	birthday
oui (wee)	yes
non (non)	no
s'il vous plait (sill-vou-play)	please
merci (mair-see)	thank you
l' instituteur (leensteetuhtuhr)	teacher
la mère (la mair)	mother
le père (luh pair)	father
la fille (la fee-yer)	girl
le garçon (luh gar-son)	boy
Comment vas-tu? (ko-mo-vahs-tew)	How are you?
Je vais bien, merci. (juh vay beyahn, mercee)	I am fine, thank you.
Comment t'appelles-tu? (koman ta-pel-tew)	What is your name?
Je m'appelle (zher ma-pel) _____.	My name is _____.
l'ours blanc (loors bl`ank)	polar bear
le phoque (luh phuk)	seal
le morse (luh mohrse)	walrus

Numbers

un (ewn)	one
deux (der)	two
trois (trwa)	three
quarte (katr)	four
cinq (sank)	five
six (sees)	six
sept (set)	seven
huit (weet)	eight
neuf (nerf)	nine
dix (dees)	ten

Colors

rouge (roojue) - red
vert (veart) - green
orange (o-range) - orange
violet (v-o-lay)- purple
blanc (blaanc) - white

noir (noare) - black
bleu (bleur) - blue
jaune (juh`an) - yellow
rose (ros) - pink
brun (broon) - brown

Days of the Week

lundi (loon-dee) - Monday
mardi (mar-dee) - Tuesday
mercredi (mare-cra-dee) - Wednesday
jeudi (ju-dee) - Thursday

vendredi (vaugnh-dra-dee) - Friday
samedi (s`am-`a-dee) - Saturday
dimanche (de-maunche) - Sunday

Canadian Recipes

Snowballs or Ice Cream with Maple Topping

Directions:
Make a snowball or take one cup of vanilla ice cream and mold into a ball. Heat maple syrup and pour over the snow or ice cream. Serve in bowls and top with chopped nuts.

Canadian Baked Blueberry Dessert

Ingredients:
1 16 oz. package frozen blueberries (or fresh blueberries)
1 ½ tablespoons lemon juice
2 teaspoons cornstarch
1 cup packed brown sugar (divided in half)
½ cup flour
⅔ cup quick-cooking oats
¼ teaspoon salt
⅓ cup margarine

Directions:
In an ungreased casserole dish, toss blueberries with lemon juice. In a separate bowl, mix cornstarch with ½ cup of brown sugar. Stir into the blueberries. Mix flour, oats, the remainder of the brown sugar (½ cup), and salt. Cut in margarine with a fork and sprinkle the mixture over the blueberries. Bake uncovered at 350° for 45 minutes or until blueberries are bubbly and the topping is light brown. Serve warm with snowballs or vanilla ice cream balls.

Learn more about the Canadian Inuits. Although many Inuits live in modern homes, some Inuits who live near the arctic region live in homes called igloos. Most of us think of igloos as houses made from ice blocks, but Inuits call tents, sod houses, etc., igloos as well. Igloos built of ice are used in the winter. Have your class create models of igloos from sugar cubes, or students can make tents from heavy cloth. Igloos can also be made by ripping small pieces of white paper and gluing them onto blue construction paper in the shape of an igloo. The children can write facts about the Inuits and attach them to their igloos. Ask your class, "In what ways have the Inuits adapted their life-styles to the climate of the arctic region?"

Your class can simulate ice hockey by playing floor hockey in the gymnasium (get your P. E. teacher involved). If you live in a city that has an NHL or minor league hockey team, have an evening out with your class and their parents to watch a very exciting sport.

In cooperative groups or with a partner, have the students pick a Canadian province or territory to study. Discover more about the geography, the people, products farmed and manufactured, and other interesting facts about the provinces and territories. This activity will be a great opportunity for the students to give oral reports. Encourage students to use visual aids in their reports.

Canada is privileged to experience the aurora borealis, also known as the northern lights. Have your students research the aurora borealis to find out what scientists have learned about it and when it occurs. The Inuits have various myths and tales that explain the phenomenon. One Inuit tale says they are reflections of whales thrashing in the waves. Another tale says that the aurora borealis is the spirits of Inuit ancestors or the vapors of northern volcanoes. Have your students devise their own creative explanations for the aurora borealis.

In the province of British Columbia, the residents still practice the British custom of High Tea. Serve tea with little cakes, crackers, and cookies. Take this opportunity to teach a lesson on table manners. Host a formal affair.

The Flag of Canada

Canada

Name _____

Canadian Crossword

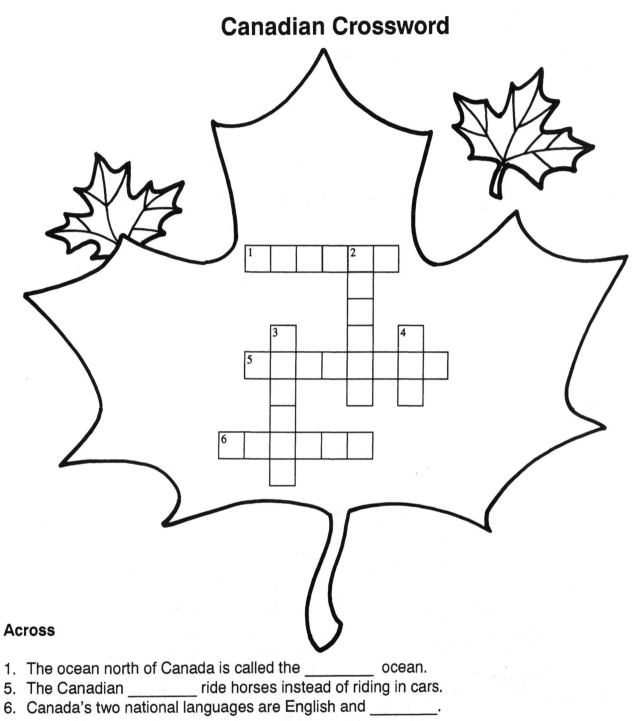

Across

1. The ocean north of Canada is called the _____ ocean.
5. The Canadian _____ ride horses instead of riding in cars.
6. Canada's two national languages are English and _____.

Down

2. Native Canadians are Indians and _____.
3. Ice _____ is Canada's most popular sport.
4. Canada has _____ provinces.

Teacher Resources

Andrews, Jan. *Very Last First Time.* Groundwood Books, 2003.

Blades, Ann. *Mary of Mile 18.* Tundra Books, 2001.

Bowers, Vivien. *Wow Canada!: Exploring This Land from Coast to Coast to Coast.* Maple Tree Press, 1999.

Greenwood, Barbara. *The Kids Book of Canada.* Kids Can Press, 1998.

Holling, Clancy. *Paddle-to-the Sea.* Houghton Mifflin, 2001.

Kalman, Bobbie. *Canada: The Culture.* Crabtree Publishing Co., 1997.

Landau, Elaine. *Canada (True Books).* Children's Press, 2000.

Marsh, Carol. *My First Book About Canada.* Gallopade International, 2001.

Moak, Allan. *A Big City ABC.* Tundra Books, 2002.

Moore, Christopher. *The Big Book of Canada: Exploring the Provinces and Territories.* Tundra Books, 2002.

Tames, Richard. *Journey Through Canada.* Troll Associates, 1991.

Ward, Lynd. *The Biggest Bear.* Sagebrush, 1999.

Waterton, Betty. *Pettranella.* Groundwood Books, 2003.

Last Stop...United States

Area: 3,618,770 sq. miles
Capital City: Washington, D.C.
Population: 295,734,134
Main Language: English
Main Religions: Protestantism and
                Roman Catholicism
Currency: American Dollar
Government: Federal Republic
Flag:

Congress has not given an official interpretation of the colors, but it is thought that red, white, and blue were chosen because they are the colors in the British flag. The thirteen stripes represent the original thirteen colonies. The fifty white stars stand for the fifty states that make up the nation. One of the flag's nicknames is Old Glory.

For Your Information

The United States consists of fifty states. Alaska and Hawaii are the only two states not connected to the United States mainland. The geography of the United States is very diverse. Land features include swamps, deserts, mountains, forests, coastlines, canyons, and volcano craters. The United States has a vast amount of fertile land and many natural resources.

In 1492, Christopher Columbus is said to have discovered the Americas. However, the land was already inhabited by natives who had lived in America for thousands of years. As the United States expanded, native Americans were driven off their land. Today, many native Americans live on reservations set up by the United States government.

The United States has often been referred to as a "melting pot" because people of many races make the United States their home. But maybe a "salad bowl" is a better term since all the races are allowed to maintain and contribute their unique cultures to the whole of the country. Unlike a melting pot, cultures in the United States do not lose their distinct qualities when blended with other cultures to form the whole country.

Fascinating Facts

Many of the states in America have names of Indian origin. For example, Iowa comes from the Indian word **Ayuhwa** meaning "sleepy one." Mississippi comes from the Indian word **misi**, meaning "big," and **sipi**, meaning "river." Wisconsin acquired its name from the Indian word **wishkonsing**, meaning "place of the beaver."

The "D. C." in Washington, D. C., stands for District of Columbia. The district was named for Christopher Columbus, and the city was named for George Washington.

The Washington Monument in Washington, D. C., sinks into the earth six inches every year.

George Washington was the only United States president who did not live in the White House.

Virginia has been home to the largest number of presidents, eight in all, including George Washington.

The flag of the United States is the only flag in the world to be the subject of a national anthem, and it was the first flag to be placed on the moon (July 20, 1969).

The lowest point in the United States is Death Valley, California, which is 282 feet below sea level. One summer the temperature reached 134° F.

It is possible to stand in four states at the same time. The Four Corners of Arizona, New Mexico, Colorado, and Utah is the only place where the corners of four states touch.

Missouri and Tennessee are each surrounded by eight other states, more than any other state.

Alaska is the largest but least populated state.

The tallest building in North America is the Sears Tower. It is located in Chicago, Illinois. It is 1,450 feet tall (110 stories).

The United States' national bird was almost a turkey. Benjamin Franklin proposed that the turkey be the national bird because it was a true native of the country. In 1782, it was finally decided that the bald eagle, which is unique to North America, would be the choice.

American Southwest Amigo Dip

Ingredients list one:
8 oz. cream cheese
½ cup sour cream
2 tablespoons milk
1 teaspoon lemon
1 teaspoon chili powder
2 ripe avocados, peeled and cut into small chunks

Ingredients list two:
1-2 cups shredded lettuce
2 tomatoes, diced
½ cup diced green onions
1-2 cups shredded cheddar cheese
1 jar mild salsa sauce

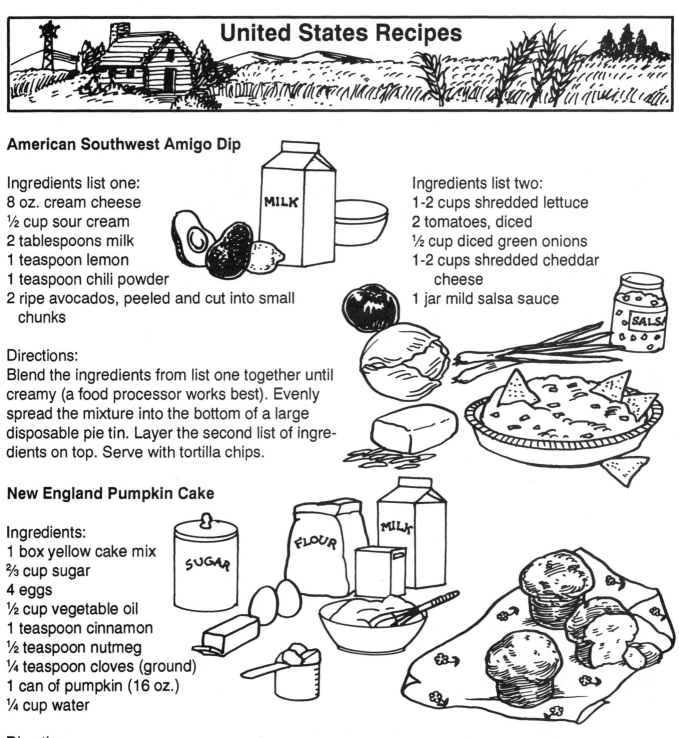

Directions:
Blend the ingredients from list one together until creamy (a food processor works best). Evenly spread the mixture into the bottom of a large disposable pie tin. Layer the second list of ingredients on top. Serve with tortilla chips.

New England Pumpkin Cake

Ingredients:
1 box yellow cake mix
⅔ cup sugar
4 eggs
½ cup vegetable oil
1 teaspoon cinnamon
½ teaspoon nutmeg
¼ teaspoon cloves (ground)
1 can of pumpkin (16 oz.)
¼ cup water

Directions:
Combine all dry ingredients in a large mixing bowl. Add eggs and stir them into the mixture. Add water and oil. Beat on low speed until well blended. Add the pumpkin. Blend on low speed until smooth. Pour into a greased bundt ban and bake at 350˚ for one hour.

Mountain Trail Mix

Ingredients:
raisins
chocolate candies
pretzels
peanuts
chocolate chips
granola
coconut
dried fruit
cereal

Directions:
Depending on the taste you want, use as much or as little of each ingredient. Mix all ingredients in a big bowl. Put individual servings in small paper cups. This recipe is also a good measuring activity if you involve your students in its preparation.

Southern Cheese Grits Casserole

Ingredients:
6 cups water
2 ½ teaspoons salt
1 ½ cups quick-cooking grits, uncooked
½ cup butter or margarine
1 cup cheddar cheese, cubed
3 eggs, separated
paprika

Directions:
Combine the water and salt in a four-quart dish or Dutch oven. Boil water, then stir the grits in slowly. Cook over low heat, stirring constantly until thickened. Remove from heat. Stir in butter and cheese until the cheese melts. Stir in the egg yolks. Beat egg whites until stiff, fold into the cheese mixture, and pour into a greased three-quart casserole dish. Sprinkle with paprika. Bake at 350° for 30-40 minutes. Serves about 12.

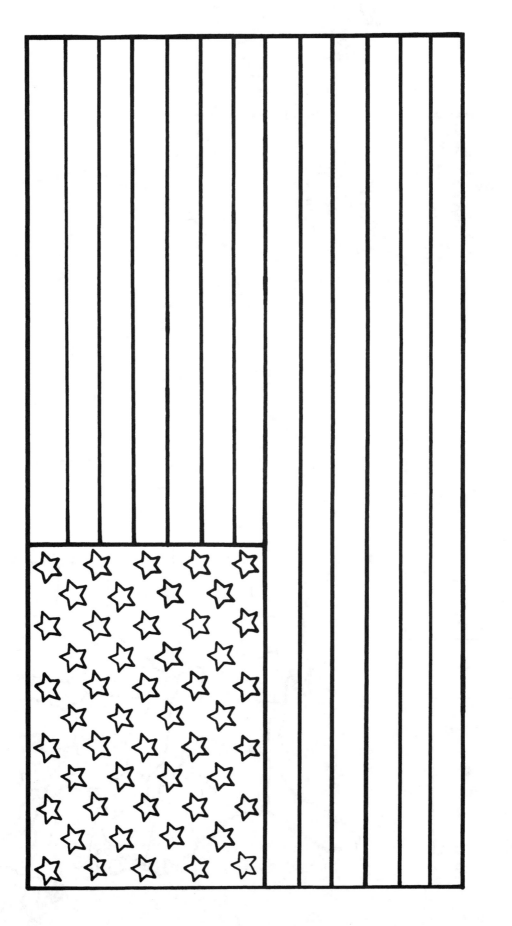

The Flag of the United States

The United States

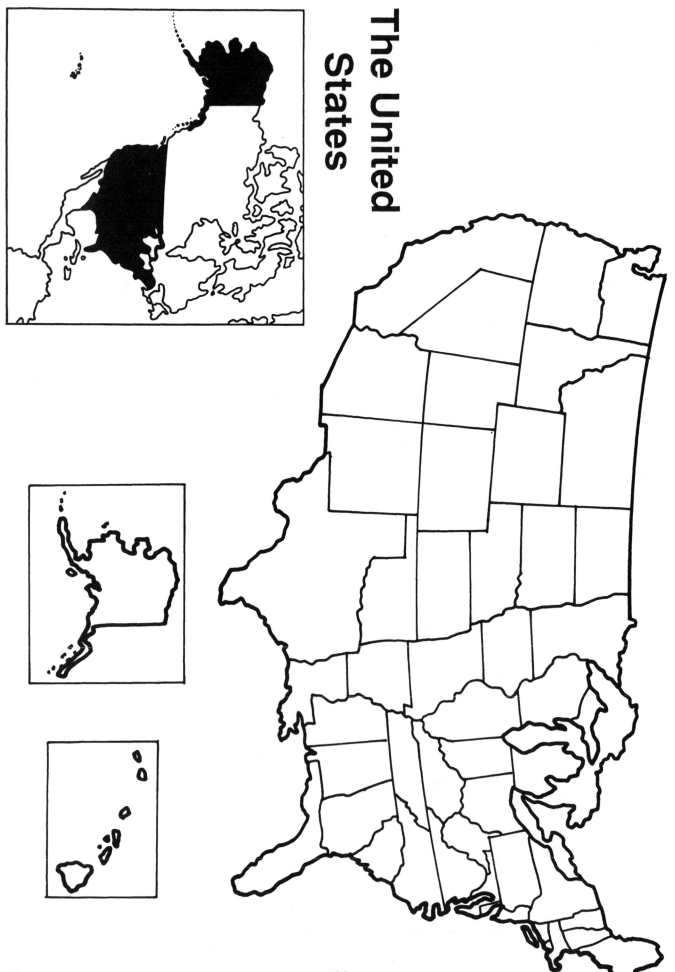

108

American Crossword

Directions: Read the questions and fill in the words in the Liberty Bell.

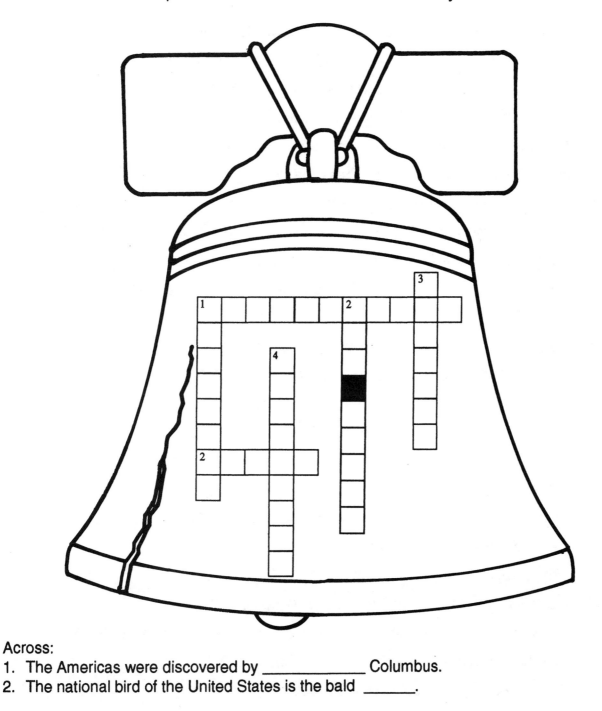

Across:
1. The Americas were discovered by _____ Columbus.
2. The national bird of the United States is the bald _____.

Down:
1. The United States began as thirteen _____.
2. The nickname of the American flag is _____ _____.
3. America is often referred to as a _____ pot.
4. In 1620, the Pilgrims set sail on the _____.

Teacher Resources

Aliki. *Corn is Maize: The Gift of the Indians.* Sagebrush, 1999.

Challe, Gary. *Yankee Doodle.* DK Publishing, 1993.

dePaola, Tomie. *The Legend of the Bluebonnet.* Putnam Juvenile, 1996.

dePaola, Tomie. *The Legend of the Indian Paintbrush.* Putnam Juvenile, 1996.

Gibbons, Gail. *Beacons of Light: Lighthouse.* Morrow Junior Books, 1990.

Goble, Paul. *The Girl Who Loved Wild Horses.* Aladdin, 1993.

Gray, Nigel. *A Country Far Away.* Anderson Pr. Ltd., 1999.

Harshman, Marc. *A Little Excitement.* Quarrier Press, 2002.

Isadora, Rachel. *Ben's Trumpet.* HarperTrophy, 1991.

Jones, Rebecca C. *The Biggest (and Best) Flag That Ever Flew.* Cornell Maritime Press, 1988.

Kellogg, Steven. *Johnny Appleseed: A Tall Tale.* Morrow, 1988.

Key, Francis Scott. *The Star Spangled Banner.* Random House Books for Young Readers, 2002.

Maestro, Betsy. *The Story of the Statue of Liberty.* HarperTrophy, 1989.

Martin, Bill. *Knots on a Counting Rope.* Henry Holt & Co., 1997.

McDermott, Gerald. *Arrow to the Sun: A Pueblo Indian Tale.* Viking, 2004.

Noble, Trinka Hakes. *Meanwhile Back at the Ranch.* Puffin Books, 1992.

Quiri, Patricia Ryan. *The Bald Eagle (True Books).* Children's Press, 1998.

Quiri, Patricia Ryan. *The Statue of Liberty (True Books).* Children's Press, 1998.

Rylant, Cynthia. *The Relatives Came.* Aladdin, 1993.

Rylant, Cynthia. *When I Was Young in the Mountains.* Puffin Books, 1993.

Schoenherr, John. *Bear.* Paperstar Books, 1991.

Scholastic, Inc. *The Pledge of Allegiance.* Scholastic, 2001.

Seattle, Chief and Jeffers, Susan. *Brother Eagle, Sister Sky.* Dial, 1991.

Shea, Pegi Dietz. *Liberty Rising: The Story of the Statue of Liberty.* Henry Holt & Co., 2005.

Troughton, Joanna. *How Rabbit Stole the Fire.* Gardners Books, 1994.

Van Allsburg, Chris. *The Stranger.* Houghton Mifflin, 1986.

Waters, Kate. *Sarah Morton's Day: A Day in the Life of a Pilgrim Girl.* Scholastic, 1993.

Yorinks, Adrienne. *Quilt of States: Piecing Together America.* National Geographic Children's Books, 2005.

Children of the World

Directions: Have the children sit in a circle as they sing along with the song. Discuss different ways of saying hello in various languages. Shake hands with each child as you use different ways to say hello. The music for this song can be found on *Children of the World* by Georgiana Stewart (published by Kimbo Educational Records, Long Beach, NJ 1991).

Children of the world
Anywhere they go,
Children of the world
Just smile and say hello.
They shake a friendly hand
And seem to understand,
Children of the world
Together learn and grow.
Say hello, "Hello"
Say hello, "Hello"
Say hello, make a new friend today.

(Repeat)

*Permission granted for use of above lyrics by Kimbo Educational Records, Long Beach, NJ.

Congratulations,

On Your Flight Around the World!